POLITICAL CONSCIENCE

Rediscovering Values in American Politics

Michael J. McMurray

A Political Conscience

Copyright © 2019 Michael J. McMurray

All scripture references, unless otherwise stated, are taken from The Holy Bible, King James Version, digital application, app3daily, updated 20 October 2019.

All Rights Reserved
No part of this publication may be reproduced, stored in a retrievable system, or transmitted by any means: electronic, mechanical, photocopy, recording, or otherwise, without the expressed written permission from the publisher, except in the case of brief quotations cited in critical articles or reviews.

Additional Credits:

Edited By: Chad Pettit
Cover Artwork: Pixelstudio: pixelstudio
Photography: Melissa Barrow Photography: https://www.facebook.com/MelissaBarrowPhotography/

Contents

Acknowledgments 5

Preface 7

Chapter 1:   The Moral Dilemma 11

Chapter 2:   "To Be or Not to Be?" 24

Chapter 3:   "Welcome Home" 36

Chapter 4:   "Book 'em, Danno" 49

Chapter 5:   Department of Defense? 59

Chapter 6:   The War for Social Justice 77

Chapter 7:   Jesus is not a Socialist 96

Chapter 8:   Conclusion 112

References 117

Acknowledgments

To: my parents, William and Gloria McMurray. Thank you for setting the foundation in me to become the man I am today. Thank you for being the providers I needed and setting the example of what love truly is.

To: my wife, Jennifer, and my kids, Sean, Natalie, and Ethan. Thank you for your faithfulness to our God and to our family. Y'all have made it very easy to be your husband and father. I love each and every one of you with all my heart

To: My future grandchildren. I want to leave you with a better United States than the one I was born into. It was already a great nation. But I was always taught to "leave it better than you found it." My desire of for all of you, your children, grand children and so on to grow up in an even better one than I did.

Preface

I have always been a politically conscious person. Even as a young boy, I enjoyed listening to the politically charged, spirited debates between my parents and their friends. The discussions they had while playing cards at the kitchen table or standing around the barbecue pit fascinated my young mind. I would sit and listen to all of the adults sharing their opinions about everything from Soviet nuclear policy to hunters in the upper peninsula of Michigan having the right to hunt deer out of season so they could feed their families. Statements like, "I agree with you on this point but disagree with you on this part" were staples of conversations. These conversations were a regular occurrence in the McMurray house. This was one of the many fascinating aspects of growing up as a "Cold War Kid" living on a Strategic Air Command Air Force Base.

Listening to my parents and their friends discuss the foreign policies of countries, such as the former Soviet Union, Iran, Israel, Europe, Cuba, as well as many other South American nations, helped cultivate in me a mature political thought process at a young age. My mom and dad were not political hard-liners on either side of the aisle. I remember going over to my parents' friends' homes and seeing some very aggressive propaganda concerning Cold War relations with communist countries. One poster–which hung in a neighbor's basement–had Mickey Mouse "flipping the bird" with the caption: "Up yours Iran!" When I asked my parents about posters like these, they were always very gracious in their response. They would say, "Michael, we agree that communism is wrong and will fight against it if we need to. But we will not hold hatred in our hearts toward anyone simply because we may disagree." The evidence of this moral position they held was in the fact that they would continue to work and socialize with those same people they had disagreed with the night before.

So, why bother writing a book on having a political conscience? The answer is relatively simple. We live in a time of such political division that friendships have been dissolved and family members no longer communicate with one another. Politics has become an all or nothing venture. If a self-proclaimed Republican deviates from the party line, that person is branded as a heretic, or worse, a Democrat. And the same is true of those on the left side of the aisle. Deviate just one iota from the party line and you will be blackballed. These days, fear on both sides is determining the direction of America's political future.

These extreme ideologies from both parties are void of any compassion, yet both sides try to claim the moral high ground as the keepers of all things compassionate and logical. The pages that follow are not an endorsement of any party's political positions. Rather, this book is an academic exercise attempting to develop the method by which we, as a society, measure individuals seeking to lead our great country, regardless of what level of government or capacity they may wish to serve.

As a citizen of this great country, I am concerned with the direction that our nation's leaders are directing the United States. This book seeks to discuss what authorities should determine the formation of our laws by highlighting some of the more controversial topics at the forefront of our nation's political narrative. Should science be the soul reference through which we develop laws? With an overwhelming theological representation throughout our country, should we base our laws on religious texts? As the growing social media outlets reach a broader range of people globally, should social engineering be the greatest component for law makers to consider when drafting legislation? Each chapter will discuss the issues within the given topic of the chapter, a discussion of both parties' talking points of the topic, as well as provide recommendations for future legislation or the reduction of legislative measures to restore American to the representative republic she was intended to be.

1

THE MORAL DILEMMA

> *That we henceforth being no more children, tossed to and from, and carried about with every wind of doctrine, by the sleight of man, and cunning craftiness, whereby they lie in wait to deceive.*
>
> *Ephesians 4: 14*

Except for the 1960s, the American social landscape is more politically charged today than perhaps any other time in history. On the left side of the political aisle, much of the belief is fueled by more emotion than fact or truth. On the right, it is exactly the opposite. Facts rule the day, leaving little room for compassion. Yet, each side holds the belief that it is the keeper of the moral high ground. So who is correct, and how is the average American citizen supposed to choose from two polarized political ideologies? In order to answer that question, individuals must first understand what their own, personal beliefs are and be able to maturely articulate them without hatred toward contrary beliefs. In short, just because we may not agree, doesn't mean I should hate you or, worse, actively try to destroy you.

As a Warrant Officer in the United States Army I was often asked to teach Warrant Officer Professional Growth and Development (WOPD) classes to other junior warrant officers. Most of the classes focused on individual and collective tasks: how to get better at the technical and tactical aspects of our craft. After about the fifth year of teaching three classes a year, I felt that as a senior Warrant Officer I could offer more than a series of steps to developing a targeting packet to align with targeting methodology. There was something fundamentally lacking when it came to how we were presenting information to our leadership. So I developed a WOPD that examined the topic: "What to do if you disagree with your leadership." In that presentation I asked one simple question: Is there such a thing as a moral Dilemma?

I posed this question to fifty of the brightest Targeting Warrant Officers in the United States Army. Universally, they agreed that there are moral dilemmas. After their affirmation to the question, I would then ask, "Then why does the United States Army or any other organization have guidelines of behavior?" The U.S. Army has the Code of Conduct and the Core Values. These two documents strive to establish acceptable ways by which Soldiers and leaders are to conduct themselves. They also serve to assist leadership in developing decision making strategies consistent with the organization's moral foundation. At the heart of this debate is a deep, underlying conflict: Do we follow principles over preference or vice versa?

A POLITICAL CONSCIENCE

I attended my twenty-year high school reunion a few years back. This was a two-day event, beginning with a casual meet-and-greet on a Friday night and ending on Saturday night with a formal dinner. Arriving at the casual meet-and-greet, I must say I was a little nervous. However, once we all started reintroducing ourselves, conversations began to flow more casually. It was a wonderful time catching up with old friends and learning about old acquaintances. As the conversation and alcohol began to flow more rapidly, an old friend approached me and said, "Mike, man, I got this moral dilemma. Jane Doe (name changed to protect the innocent– (who happened to be married) wants to sleep with me."

That is when the concept of the illusion of a moral dilemma donned on me, and I responded with the following statement. "John Doe (name changed), there is no dilemma here. If your morals state it's OK to sleep with a married woman, then by all means go. If they do not, then you have your answer, already." I am thankful he made the right decision and decided not to sleep with another man's wife. You see, he could have, and it is likely that Jane Doe's husband would have never known. But that really isn't the point, is it? Just because someone may not find out does not make it right. When I applied for the Sandoval County Detention Center, I was asked in the interview what ethics means to me. My response was a resounding, "Doing what's right even when no one is watching".

There are no moral dilemmas, provided our principles are grounded in truth and thought through maturely and delivered with compassion. The dilemma only arises when the organization's principles might be in conflict with one's personal principles. So does one side with the organization or hold to his or her own principles? In this socially conscience, politically divisive, social media driven age, many individuals abandon their personal principles for the sake of the organization. For the purpose of this book, that means a political party. This is due to the fact many people allow their political affiliation to determine their beliefs rather than determine what is true and hold the political parties accountable to the truth.

We as a society are bombarded with the new age philosophy of "Live Your Truth." I disagree with this concept from a fundamental perspective. There is not just "your truth." There are absolutes in the world. There is right, and there is wrong. To live "your truth" is to without compassion prevent someone else from living his or her truth. "The Truth" is measurable, knowable, and trustworthy; and it can be displayed with a tremendous amount of compassion. Hate filled rhetoric, fueled by emotion and factual decision making void of compassion is equally as harmful to the American political landscape.

Much of what is spoken about today is America's greatness. "Make America Great Again," or "America has always been great," and/or "America was never great." Depending on one's perspective, any one of these statements could be true. I personally believe America has always been great, but if I was to ask an African American who grew up during the Jim Crow era, he or she would certainly have a different perspective on America's greatness. So who is right, and who is wrong? Let's look at a few other examples.

Many historians believe the British Empire was a great super power. Ask someone living in India in the 1930s and 1940s just how "great" the British Empire was, and they might have a different opinion. Persia was another so-called great empire. No one is alive today to ask, but I would venture a guess that the Babylonians were none-to-happy with the "greatness" of the Persian Empire. Then of course, we have Alexander the Great. I mean, "great' is in his name, right? So he must be right for conquering the entire known world at the time? One need only ask King Darius III to understand not everyone believes what Alexander the Great did was morally justified.

The more pertinent question to ask is, "Does greatness equal uprightness?" It does not matter if America is great if what we do is not moral. If the decisions our leaders make are not rooted in truth and manifested through compassion, we have failed to elect the best leaders for our nation. The truth stands on its own merit. The personality traits of our leadership determine the level of compassion any given law is implemented. Where conflict arises with this concept is in what constitutes compassion?

Compassion is seeing a need of the people, gaining knowledge of the situation, and applying wisdom so that the need is met. The misunderstanding here is that most Americans, on the left and right side of the political aisle, believe compassion is getting what they want. The problem with this thinking is that, when one group gets what it wants, the inevitable second and third order effects are other groups being denied what they want. It is this false definition of compassion that allows both sides to claim the moral victory. It is also why the actual problems never get resolved. It is the proverbial, "I am taking my ball and going home." If you don't play my way, then nobody gets to play at all. And the inability for our nation's leaders to determine what it means to be compassionate has led to moral ambiguity. If everyone is simply doing what is right in their own eyes, nothing anyone is doing is right.

During my third deployment to Iraq– my second as a Warrant Officer–I began hearing the term Acceptable Levels of Corruption (ALC). What was not defined was what those levels were. Because we were purposefully accepting corruption, no leader in his or her right mind was going to put down on paper what acceptable levels of corruption were. That would mean we were admitting to playing the game without any moral guidelines. But the catch twenty-two of it was that, by not defining it, leaders were left to determine their own thresholds, and there were no checks and balances to prevent someone from going too far. The only real determination of a violation was when the next higher ranking commander was embarrassed by the actions of his subordinate commander. The resulting punishment was someone being relieved of command. This created a situation in which many subordinate commanders were hesitant to make decisions for fear of getting relieved of command simply by embarrassing their leadership. Yet, the subordinate commanders never really knew what the standard of conduct was.

I am not saying this concept has only begun to rear its ugly head recently. I am saying that we have become so accepting of corruption that we defend it when it fits our political ideologies. By way of example, when a Democrat politician gets caught cheating on his spouse, the Republicans are all hands-across-America to end the offending politician's career. Yet, when it is a Republican that commits the same offense, the response is, "What people do on their time has nothing to do with their ability to lead." It was through this failed concept that I abandoned the two-party political system. I used to think this system was helpful in deciding who was right and who was wrong. Sadly, this is no longer the case. Each side has become morally ambiguous.

Another example of this is when Josh Duggar's molestation allegations surfaced. When The Right began to defend the boy's actions and those of his parents, I was appalled. Some of the people who were coming to the defense of this atrocious behavior were leaders in the Christian community. I could not believe that the truth was being abandoned for the sake of saving political face. "No way are we going to let The Left shame us. So we will just claim the moral high ground and mock them" became the information campaign to save the Duggar family's reputation. This had nothing to do with the truth. It was after this that I abandoned the Republican Party. And again, during the 2016 Presidential campaign, The Right would defend vulgar behavior when the tapes surfaced of President Trump making vulgar comments about the treatment of women only for The Right to defend the statements by making fun of The Left and their "Witch Hunts." Defense of these behaviors is the direct result of moral ambiguity developing the concept of acceptable levels of corruption.

Under the current two-party system, Acceptable Levels of Corruption has been allowed not only to gain a foothold but has become the way of doing business. What is left is the "My corruption is not as bad as your corruption" syndrome. The symptom is easy to diagnose. It manifests itself in the response of: "I can lie, cheat, and steal because my ends are more moral than yours." Defense of immoral and out right illegal behavior by default negates any political party from claiming the moral high ground. Do the ends really justify the means?

The ends can never justify the means if the means seek to discount love, faith, hope, charity, and sacrifice. In 1 Corinthians 13, the Apostle Paul writes to the Church at Corinth to do all things through charity. Verses one through three tells us that if we do anything and do not have charity, it profits nothing. The Bible is very clear. The way in which we conduct ourselves has everything to do with the uprightness of the outcome. So robbing from Peter to pay Paul does not justify the robbery. This truth will become very important later on in the book when we discuss the nature of certain governing philosophies. Understanding the why of our nation's leaders is vitally important to understanding the heart of their decision making process.

> "Words may show you a man's wit, but actions his meaning."
>
> –Benjamin Franklin.

I am unaffected by the rhetoric of the modern politician. I am more concerned with what the individuals are doing and how they are getting it done. As stated above: lying, cheating, and stealing to get the job done destroys the outcome. The principle here is that, as decision makers, the way in which we do things must be done through charity. The constant battle between the perceived moral high ground continues to shift. This continued shifting of the moral high ground is proof neither side of the political aisle has a desire to conduct itself uprightly. Rather, both sides seek to dupe the American people in order to achieve their own personal agendas. With the goal of those agendas failing to protect the American people and the rights endowed to them by their creator.

How does one shape a world view that will assist him or her in a decision making process that will remove the moral dilemma and allow for compassion while behaving charitably? The short answer is: purposefully. It will not come by accident. In order to develop any sort of process, it must be planned with the end goal of getting to the truth. Next, develop the tools and traits necessary to implement the decision with compassion. My world view is first established through a solid foundation and then guided by principles tied to the foundation. These two tenets then provide guidance on how my ideas and beliefs manifest themselves. Each step in the process must be purposeful and deliberate. Simply put, establish my foundation in the truth, develop principles of action tied to those truths, and then manifest my behaviors so people will see the truth in action.

The foundation which shapes my world view is the Bible. The principles of love, charity, compassion, sacrifice, patience, knowledge, wisdom, and truth are what I use to shape every decision I make. This is true from the kind of husband I am to the way my wife and I raise our three kids to the way I conduct myself at work or even my hobbies. These tenets also shape the way in which I vote for my nation's leaders. They ensure that, when faced with a difficult decision, I am guided to an outcome of truth.

Many political pundits and socially conscience voters question the validity of using the Bible as a source of moral guidance. This is due to the supposed endorsement of slavery in the scriptures. God, in no instance in scripture, endorses or approves slavery. As I studied this topic for this book and read through the Bible, I could not find any

THE MORAL DILEMMA

reference where God was the initiator of a slave agreement. What we do read in scripture is God instituting rules for slavery. This may seem like a contradiction or even an excuse for slavery. I encourage you to keep reading and allow this thought to mature.

In Matthew chapter nineteen, Jesus tells the Pharisees that Moses authorized the divorce for the Israelites because of the "hardness of their hearts." He then tells them that this was not the way it was meant to be. God had a different plan. In I Samuel chapter one, the Israelites ask God for a king to rule over them. God expresses His desire to be the only king to rule over them. Because of their persistence, God grants them a king.

In each of these examples we see God granting man what they want, even when it goes against what He has designed for His creation. After giving man what he wants, God then established rules for how they are to handle divorce and how the king should rule in order to rule righteously. As we have seen through history, however, we humans can be extremely cruel to our fellow man. Divorce has become commonplace and for reasons as simple as the two people no longer liking one another. Kings, or rulers of nations, have time and time again abused their power. To list all of the world leaders who have committed crimes against humanity and what they have done would require volumes of books. Even with all of the inconsistency with man's behavior, people are still getting married, and people are still asking the government to fix their problems.

The first mention of slavery is when the Israelites became slave to Egypt. This was not mandated by God but by the ruler of Egypt: Pharaoh. Then, after four-hundred years of slavery, they were delivered out of Egypt by Moses. It was man that held the first slaves. In Exodus we see it was fear of the Israelites that drove Pharaoh to take them captive. Then, as Israel was establishing itself as a nation, the surrounding nations had slaves and used them as currency. Once again it was man's indifference to his fellow man that led to slavery. It was through God's mercy toward the evil of man that rules were established to ensure that abuse of a slave was not conducted.

Exodus chapter twenty-one is where we see the first rules established for slavery. The very first mention of slavery is in reference to a barter system in which a man who has no other means to make a living can trade work for goods. There is a length of time to be indebted: six years. The evidence here shows that the slavery mentioned in the Bible is not the same slavery we have seen in our own country's history. It is also clear that slavery was never meant to be a permanent condition of the people. It was to last only a few years and then set the debtor free. This was not the slavery we had here in our country.

In Deuteronomy chapter twenty-four, God tells the nation of Israel that stealing another Israelite for the purpose of making him a slave is punishable by death. So stealing for the sole purpose to enslave is also against the Bible. In Ephesians chapter six, Paul writes concerning the relationship between a slave and his master. The slave is to obey his master and respect him. The master is to refrain from threatening the slave and to respect him as well. The slavery written of in the Bible is a working slavery designed with an end in sight. That end was to ensure the eventual freedom of the slave. According to the Bible, a man can volunteer to remain a slave for life, but this was completely voluntary.

The slavery we have seen in modern history is not synonymous with the slavery we see in the Bible. A complete study of this topic does show that even the slavery of the Bible was not fair but it was not brutal, either. The slavery rules were established because of man's wickedness toward man. This was God extending His grace to protect the one enslaved. The goal of the slavery rules: to see the slave eventually freed. Where most modern political and theological commentators have with slavery in the Bible is the word obey. In a day where "live your own truth" is the tag line, to obey is egregious to that ideology. It does not mean to obey is wrong or a weak character trait. Those who have ever been a boss, leader, or supervisor want their employees to obey. It creates an environment of good order and discipline. How the Bible has ensured good order and discipline in my own life is as a Soldier and leader in the U.S. Army. The following story is exactly why I know the Bible can be used as a source of moral guidance.

While stationed at Fort Carson, Colorado, I was one of five Targeting Officers at the 4th Infantry Division Headquarters. The story that is about to follow is in no way a reflection of the 4ID chain of command's standard of conduct. This is a story about the people involved.

It was a Friday morning, and those of us in the office were talking about our weekend plans. One officer, who came in at the tail end of the conversation, asked what everyone was doing. We all shared our plans. He was a young officer who had recently gone through a divorce. He was looking to unwind from a hard week of work on a division staff and asked me if I wanted to go to a strip club. Before I even had a chance to get my answer out, the rest of the Soldiers present began to laugh. This officer, being relatively new to the staff, was unaware of my beliefs, so he was quite puzzled at all the laughter. That is when another fellow warrant officer spoke up and advised the young officer that I was a Christian and did not go to places like that.

There are a few things to observe here. First, my beliefs were well known, protected me from any awkward confrontation, and eliminated the moral dilemma. Second, just because he asked me to go does not mean I should have been offended and begun to preach hell-fire and brimstone at him. His asking me to go does not make me guilty of going. It is not a sin to be tempted. The third observation is that he did not get offended because I did not want to go. He understood my beliefs. He clearly did not agree with them but was not going to spend the rest of his time mocking me into changing what I believed.

Having a foundation to shape your world view and purposefully and deliberately working out your beliefs is paramount to a mature decision making process. As we begin to examine some of the more controversial subjects of our current political and social architecture, we will see how not establishing and knowing what we believe leads to indecisiveness and outright wrong decisions. The greatest tragedy is that, on the political scale, it is an entire nation and its people who are affected. We have a great responsibility in this representative republic to ensure that our leadership seeks the uprightness rather than greatness. The greatest political power on earth is truth in the heart of a righteous man.

2

"To Be or Not to Be?"

"For the life of the flesh is in the blood: and I have given it to you upon the alter to make an atonement for your souls: for it is the blood that maketh an atonement for the soul."

Leviticus 17:11

There is no greater revelation in the heart of man than how we treat the most innocent and vulnerable among us. There is no one more innocent and vulnerable than an unborn child. An unborn child is so vulnerable to the threats of the outside world; it must grow in a well-protected environment. [1] The protective environment consists of the wall of the uterus, the yolk sac, amniotic fluid, the uterus itself, and of course, the mother's

---

[1] The endowment for Human Development, *Prenatal Form and Function – The Making of an Earth Suit* (on-line article)

body. All of this is provided to ensure the vulnerable life growing inside the mother has the best chance for survival.

The fertilized embryo is so fragile that it is estimated that [2] about half of all fertilized eggs fail to attach to the wall of the uterus and are simply discarded through the natural menstrual cycle. Many women never even know they are pregnant. This fact will become important later on in this chapter as we seek to define what our moral foundation should be in this country concerning the subject of abortion. How can one conceive the idea that it is acceptable in a modern society for the one designed to care for such a vulnerable life would seek to end it prematurely through the violence of an abortion?

This chapter is not an exhaustive study on the science and biology of how life begins, nor is it a deep-dive into the religious heart of the American conscience. This chapter looks to examine the moral foundation of the decision to conduct an abortion, as well as the laws that allow for a modern society to see abortions as viable medical procedures for an unwanted pregnancy. What drives lawmakers to want to make laws allowing for abortions, and what would drive a person to want to kill her unborn child? This chapter will also look to answer the question of when life begins and compare the truth to the ideologies of our two most predominant political parties.

Is it even necessary to have an abortion, today? With all of the advancements in medicine and technology, are we not, as a civilized society, obligated to seek more humane ways to treat one other? Should we not discover more mature and compassionate ways to resolve our

---

[2] Cunningham FG, MacDonald PC, Gant NF, et al. 1997. *Williams Obstetrics, 20th ed.* Stamford: Appleton and Lange.

differences? We have used this reasoning to incorporate more humane ways of treating our prisoners. We have made laws to prevent our animals from being treated with cruelty. Yet here we stand, the greatest country on Earth, and we cannot find the reason to compassionately deal with the struggles of whether to have an abortion or whether abortion should even be legal.

Both sides of the political aisle claim to base their arguments from a scientific perspective. The Left says the baby is just a bundle of cells, and since an embryo/fetus is not sentient, it is not life. The Right says that since the cells are growing, this constitutes life. Then, when each defeats the other's scientific claims, they resort to the emotional aspect of the argument. The Left responds with, "Well you just want to tell women what to do, you misogynist." The Right counters with impassioned restatements of their original position, showing no care and concern for the women making these difficult decisions.

I can't even imagine what it must be like for a young teenage girl, who in the pressure of a passion filled night, makes a poor life choice to participate in activity that results in a pregnancy. Or even worse, the pregnancy is thrust upon a woman due to a forcible act committed against her. We, a society designated as a nation of laws, have an obligation to see the need and work to make laws compassionate concerning the mother that also protect the vulnerable, fragile life growing inside of her. Our laws should reflect this concern. This is where our moral foundation must stand.

The Left begins its argument from the firm hand of the U.S. Constitution, backed by the Supreme Court's ruling on Roe versus Wade. This is an attempt to gain the legal high ground as precedence for allowing abortions to continue.

A POLITICAL CONSCIENCE

The Left then argues that the landmark case did not go far enough in allowing what now amounts to unrestricted and late term abortions. This legal high ground is void of any care for the unborn child. More so now in allowing for the murder of a baby even after the birthing process has begun. Who will speak on behalf of the unborn child? Well, keep reading. The answer will be revealed later in this chapter.

There is a belief on The Left that the fetus has no human rights. Therefore, is not protected by the Constitution. They can say this because of their definition of life. They simply deny that the baby is a life. Thus, it is not protected under our Constitution. How can they then claim they care about life at all if they say the most innocent and most vulnerable are not even living? The answer is that they cannot. This stands in contradiction to the moral high ground argument of The Left being more compassionate than the Right. The Left is able to maintain a foothold here because the Right lacks compassion as well but more on that later. Let's continue dissecting the Left's arguments.

Then of course, the third stance they take is captured in the phrase, "My body, my choice." This is saying that, unless you have a uterus, you have no say in abortion laws. So, why call for abortions once the baby has been removed from the mother? In no way can anyone not draw the conclusion that once the baby is removed from the mother, it is no longer part of the mother's body. Therefore, it is no longer her choice. At that point it becomes murder. Why? Because of the same document the Left just claimed as the authority for allowing abortions in the first place. So, if the authority of the U.S. Constitution grants you the right for an abortion, that same document also safeguards the sanctity of human life. To kill a baby after it is born is murder. To make laws that allow for this behavior is to legalize murder, and where would the Left then draw the line?

Aside from the legal and scientific arguments previously listed here is the truth of where the Left stands on abortion, which is that it is the socially conscience duty of every American woman to agree with abortion and allow for the uninhibited participation in this activity. The evidence of this is in the "Shout your abortion" movement sweeping across major cities in the United States. Yet, leftist leaders will make statements such as, [3]"This is one of the worst possible choices that any woman and her family has to make" made by Hillary Clinton. So how can one say it is a difficult decision and then support a movement that believes it is the greatest decision a woman can make. This is yet another glaring contradiction to the Left's narrative.

Now where the Left is consistent is in its stance of not caring about the baby. It is all about the mother, and the Left will never waiver from this position. I am completely and fundamentally against such a stance. It is about the mother *and* the baby. The Left likes to invoke the worst case scenario emotion in us to get us to relent on our position or make us feel guilty about having an opinion different from theirs. My counter to this is to regulate to the worst case scenario. Do not give permission to just arbitrarily murder an unborn child.

The Right's position, on the other hand, simply states life begins at conception and to abort a pregnancy at any time beyond conception is murder. If you don't want to get pregnant, you have the personal responsibility to prevent it. Either you abstain from activities that result in pregnancy or fork over the cash to get the contraception you need.

---

[3] ABC News, Third Presidential Debate, 19 October 2016

After all, contraception is cheaper than raising a child. The Right will make concessions concerning a pregnancy as a result of rape or incest, but that is about as compassionate as it gets for the Right. It has a much more, straight forward approach to this topic.

On a social level, the Right says abortion needs to be outlawed in order to protect society. Abortion is a blight on American society. The issue then becomes, who is responsible for the prevention of life if it truly is a societal issue? Is society responsible for the distribution of conception? Then, if the contraception is used and fails, who is responsible for the care of the child? These are honest questions that deserve honest answers. There are real people out there with real struggles, and these are some of the many questions for which they need answers. So is it the responsibility of the Government to provide the answers? The simple answer is no.

I do not want the government telling me when to start and stop a family. The government needs to stay out of my home. Our founding fathers understood this. It is why we have the many laws that protect home owners from intrusive government entry. It is not the responsibility of the government to provide contraception for the prevention of pregnancy, either. However, I am not against schools and healthcare facilities handing out free contraception to anyone who visits their facilities. These are measures that help prevent the life from ever forming. There is wisdom in this.

I disagree with abortion. I do believe it to be murder and the greatest sin our nation has ever committed against the innocent. [4]Murder is the unlawful killing of a human

---

[4] 18 U.S. Code § 1111. Murder

"TO BE OR NOT TO BE?"

being with malice aforethought. One of the definitions for malice aforethought is [5]a general evil and depraved state of mind in which the person is unconcerned for the lives of others. The Left tells women abortions are safe procedures, but any activity resulting in the loss of life can in no way be seen as a safe procedure. There is no concern for the loss of life when it comes to abortion, and this, by definition, meets the legal requirement for murder. So much for the legal basis for abortion.

The question that needs to be answered is, when does life begin? Or, more importantly, when does human life begin? It is very important to understand the difference in these two questions. As we examine the science of this question, clarity will be provided to define the difference between the two. Anyone who has debated or commented on the topic of abortion has had to ask this question. Due to the legal stance the Left has on the subject, it is imperative to answer this question and then seek legislation to accept this definition.

I would like to explore the answer to when life begins both from a scientific and religious aspect. Through this discussion I will show you just how these two concepts compliment and validate each other to determine when life begins. But before I show the evidence from science and the Bible, I would like to take some time and discuss the "science" of the political parties. It is important to understand how people on each side of the political aisle view life and when they believe it begins in order to formulate an intelligent and compassionate rebuttal to either position.

---

[5] Law.com

The Right says that as long as it is growing, it is a life. And since after fertilization, the sperm and the egg form the zygote and the first cell division takes place, it would seem the Right is correct. Growth is taking place; therefore, life has begun. That seems logical enough, but we then have to ask the question as stated above. Is it a human life? No, it is not. Fungus grows, yet we do not see it as human. Just because something is growing and is alive does not make it human. I think I just heard every Republican's head explode upon reading this. And I can no doubt anticipate their responses. Fungus does not have the potential to be a human being. That would be a correct statement. However, potential does not determine outcome.

I can just hear every Republican scream the word "HERETIC" from the top of their lungs for me making that statement, so let me clarify. It is said by many guidance counselors to students, "You have a lot of potential." If the student does not apply the factors that will affect the potential outcome, he or she will never realize that potential. So even though the fertilized egg has the potential to be a human life does not mean it is human at the time of conception.

Let us reexamine the previous statement referencing the development of the embryo/fetus. We learned that science has proven that about half of all fertilized eggs fail to attach to the wall of the uterus. So was each one of those failures the death of a human being? I am sure most on the Right would now say yes. So God, who is the giver and taker of life, has orchestrated a birthing process where half of His creation is destined to die? I do not believe this to be the case.

The Left simply says it is not a life. Yet they agree that any organism which grows on Mars is proof of life on other planets. There is a glaring inconsistency with this position on what constitutes life, much less when human life begins. Thus it becomes convenient for them to simply say, "Since we have no legal definition of when life begins, we can terminate a pregnancy at any time." This is immoral. If growth of cells constitutes life on another planet, you cannot say a fertilized egg, which is clearly dividing and growing almost from the moment of conception, is not life here on Earth. The only logical conclusion I can draw from this ideology is that the Left just wants to kill unborn children. And this clearly falls within the legal definition of malice aforethought.

So, what is the truth? When does human life begin? Let's first look at the real science of embryo/fetal development. Then, let's look at what the Bible says about this subject. As we look at the evidence of these two concepts, it will become clear how both science and the Bible are in complete agreement and complement one another in such a way as to draw only one, logical conclusion.

First, the biological science. There is no development of human organs prior to the tenth day of embryo/fetal growth. This is due to the fact that no blood has been introduced into the embryo. Blood is the key ingredient to the development of human life. No blood, no human life. It really is that simple. No human organs will develop without the presence of blood. That means: no lungs, no heart, and no cardiovascular system. No human characteristics until blood is introduced and can supply the embryo with the required material to develop human characteristics. So prior to the tenth day after fertilization, there is no human life inside the mother's body.

Now for the Biblical foundation for why I believe this. As I was reading my Bible one year, I read through Leviticus, and in just about every chapter it referenced the blood. The blood was shed by animal sacrifice for the atonement of sin. In the New Testament Christ shed his own blood for our sins. It is through Christ's blood we are given eternal life, our second birth. It is not a stretch for me then to think He would use the blood to begin my first life. And in Leviticus 17:11 it states in the very first sentence, "For the life of the flesh is in the blood." I once thought as most on the Right think today. Life begins at conception. But if I tell you I believe the Bible and it clearly states life is in the blood then I have no other conclusion to draw than to say that life does not begin until blood is introduced into the embryo. The Bible is also very clear on another point when it comes to children. In Matthew 18:10 Christ states, "Take heed that ye despise not one of these little ones; for I say unto you, That in heaven their angels do always behold the face of my Father which is in heaven." Christ is telling us He has angels looking out for the little ones, and they have direct access to God Himself.

When you remove all the noise and political rhetoric, what it comes down to is answering a very simple question: When does human life begin? And as I previously stated, the Bible and science are in complete agreement. Human life is in the blood. No blood, no human life. What fascinated me most about this discovery is the built-in compassion to answer the questions of rape and incest. That is right. It is as if our Creator knew we would need this grace to give to those who are suffering. The wisdom, compassion, and forethought of our Creator blows my mind.

What then is the implication of this? Well, if a woman is raped and fears a pregnancy may result, she can seek medical attention and as part of the treatment receive medication, such as the morning after pill to ensure a pregnancy does not result. It would be the same in cases of incest. I know there will still be difficulties when it comes to providing treatment in cases of incest due to parental oversight, but we have evidence to truly do away with the killing of our unborn children. Of course, there could be issues with access to treatment for women who suffer rape.

The first issue would be an increase in false rape reports due to teenagers who have sex and simply want access to free birth control. Adults would not be exempt from the temptation to abuse this process, either. That is definitely a risk factor. This could be mitigated by schools and clinics providing medication, such as the morning after pill, to assist with the prevention of the unwanted pregnancy. The second issue would be more of a moral one. Access to medication, such as the morning after pill, may create an environment of indiscriminate and irresponsible sexual activity resulting in a culture that believes, "Since I have access to the morning after pill I don't need to use a condom." This could lead to an increase in sexually transmitted diseases as partners would decline the use of traditional contraception, like condoms, which help prevent the spread of most STDs. This, to me, represents the greatest risk to our society.

The second issue is what to do if a woman does not seek medical attention within the ten days of intercourse and a pregnancy does result. The answer is very simple. Our laws should be designed to protect human life. As such, the baby is now a human life and deserves protection. She must carry the baby to term and then she may place the baby up for adoption. ⁶With 47% of all abortions being funded by tax payers, that money could be redirected to assist in reducing the cost for adoption, another avenue by which the sanctity of human life can be preserved and cared for compassionately.

There are risks associated with any decision leaders have to make, and the decisions are not always easy. It is the responsibility of our decision makers to determine how to mitigate those risks. You will never get everyone to agree on the best way to implement the decision, but one thing that I know is that, continuing to allow abortion because we are afraid of increased false report and the potential for an increase in STDs, is to fail to protect our most innocent and vulnerable lives, the unborn children.

---

[6] Forbes Article, *Are American Taxpayers Paying for Abortion?*, 2 October 2005

3

"Welcome Home"

And if a stranger sojourn with thee in your land, ye shall not vex him. But the stranger that dwelleth with you shall be unto to you as one born among you, and thou shalt love him as thyself; for ye were strangers in the land of Egypt: I am the Lord your God

Leviticus 19:33, 34

Understanding immigration and its impact on the American social, economic, and political environment is paramount to the future success of this country. I have intentionally separated the social and economic categories for a very specific reason. As a country, we tend to collectively combine socioeconomics due to the close interaction of these concepts. However, there are greater second and third order effects related to immigration that are specific to each category and are worthy of being addressed individually to gain a mature understanding of the need for a moral foundation to our immigration laws. As with the subject of abortion, immigration is a very emotional topic. I am not seeking to discount the emotional aspect of immigrating but rather account for its emotional provocation and incorporate it as part of the reasoning for the establishment of fair entry into our American way of life.

"Give me your tired, your poor, Your huddled masses yearning to breathe free, The wretched refuse of your teeming shore. Send these, the homeless, tempest-tossed to me, I lift my lamp beside the golden door!"

The Statue of Liberty- This is a wonderful quote that demonstrates our nation's compassion for those across the globe which are suffering and in need of hope, the hope of a brighter future. Free from oppression with a chance to forge a better life. What an amazing concept: the American Dream. But should this wonderful notion be the foundation by which our immigration laws are developed?

It is with great confidence I can stipulate that the majority of Americans would agree that the above quote is indicative of the American Dream. No doubt this sentiment should be used as a guiding principle of immigration but should not be the singular ideology used to develop our laws. In principle, it means if you are poor, unwanted, mistreated and destitute and longing to be free, you will not be turned away. However, just because you are these things does not guarantee you free passage to our shores. The compassion is in the ability to become an American regardless of your helpless estate. The requirement is to assimilate to the American ideal.

First and foremost, we are a nation of laws. As described in the preamble of the Constitution, these laws "establish Justice, insure domestic Tranquility, provide for the common defense, promote the general welfare, and secure the blessings of liberty to ourselves and our posterity..." We are also a representative republic established through the democratic process. We, the people, get to determine the way in which we are governed and those whom we wish to have governing us. These laws were established through the understanding of human rights that are endowed to us by our creator. This is our national identity, and it is what should form the basis for all of our immigration laws. One need only look back through history to see the necessity for protecting our national identity.

Before we look back at the historical examples of failed immigration policies of other nations, we need to look at our own country's demographics. What makes up the human landscape of America? We have people from all walks of life. People of varying national backgrounds, economic standings, religious beliefs, and cultural backgrounds come together to make up the great American experience. The reason I use the word experience here is because, as Americans, we have to be active in creating the American way of life. It requires effort working toward a common goal, the security of freedom and liberty to our future generations. In order to provide for our future posterity, what must we prioritize in order to protect those liberties? Is it economic stability? What about the social construct of multiculturalism? Is it the safeguard of personal well-being through the laws of crime and punishment? Or, is it our national identity? Let's examine each of these topics individually to see where our priorities should lie.

Why not begin with the bottom line, the debate over economics? How does immigration affect us economically? It is well known that the United States is home to the largest immigrant population in the world. Understanding the effects on our economy is an important factor in determining the level of immigrant growth to our country. Who bears the burden of that growth? Is there even a burden to bear as it relates to immigration? Many economists, politicians, and political pundits believe the economic effects are the most important factor to consider when establishing immigration laws.

According to a study conducted by Penn Wharton of the University of Pennsylvania, [7]there is little long term effect of immigration on the U.S. economy. It also concludes that immigration leads to more innovation, a better educated workforce–which results in better skills matching with job requirements and overall economic productivity. The greatest cause of these outcomes is due to native born Americans and immigrants not competing for the same jobs, with immigrants competing amongst themselves for the lower skilled, less paying jobs in construction and agriculture. Since native born Americans are not competing for the lower paying jobs, they are hired at more lucratively paying and higher skilled jobs. The net result is that Americans are earning more money and are able to contribute to the economy more effectively through more purchasing power and as tax payers.

The issues with this study do not account for the effects of illegal immigrants into the economy. It does make mention of illegal immigration but only as an aside with no quantifiable data to back up the statement: "Immigrants in general – whether documented or undocumented – are net positive contributors to the federal budget." Yet, none of

---

[7] Penn Wharton, UPENN, Budget Model, *The Effects of Immigration on the United Sates' Economy*, 27 January 2016

the charts, graphs, or figures ever reference data concerning the calculation of the effects of illegal immigration on the economy.

An article written by Kimberly Amadeo does a much better job at accounting for the effects of both legal and illegal immigration on the U.S. economy. She uses the terms "undocumented" and "documented" to describe the status of people entering the U.S. Her findings for documented workers are similar to the findings from the Penn Wharton publication, praising the positive effects of legal immigration leading to economic growth. According to the Social Security Administration, undocumented workers account for as much as thirteen billion dollars in tax revenue.

[8]There are approximately eight million undocumented immigrants living in the United Sates, today. Of those undocumented immigrants, an estimated 3.4 million pay into social security and payroll taxes. About nine percent use food stamps, and just over one percent use welfare to assist with living expenses. This puts rough estimates of the tax payer burden around $3.5 billion to $10 billion. This broad range in estimation is due to the support provided for asylum seekers and refugees. While they are given work visas and required to pay taxes, they are exclusively cared for through government funded programs. This $3.5 to $10 billion is in stark contrast to the Right's narrative of over $135 billion in tax payer dollars to support illegal immigration. Due to the inconsistencies in reports, what is the conclusion we, as the American people, draw from this?

---

[8] *Immigration's Effects on the Economy and You*, Kimberly Amadeo, 25 January 2019

The one thing every report agrees on is that immigration stimulates economic growth. However, there is a burden to bear in the use of social programs to support immigration. Immigration also creates competition in a free market, which, again, stimulates growth. So the argument for or against immigration is not a fiscal one. The subject of the economic impact on our country is merely an emotional one designed to simply persuade voters to one side of the aisle or the other and all the while never discussing the true need for proper immigration laws and methods to enforce them.

Another topic that surrounds the immigration debate is the multicultural aspect of our country. It is true that we are a nation of immigrants. And, as a nation of immigrants, we have hundreds of different national cultures woven into the American tapestry. This creates a very unique and wonderful heritage, one that I am personally very proud of. I love traveling and telling others I am American and having the opportunity to share the unique nature of our country to those abroad who may never get the experience of seeing first-hand the true beauty of our country and its ability to absorb so many cultures while maintaining its own ideals.

A quick glance across America from coast to coast and northern to southern border reveals more than just national cultures. This wonderful country is also divided into regional cultures. Even the dialects and slang terms used in different regions of the U.S. are radically different. As an Air Force brat, my parents moved me and my two brothers around often. I was born in California, braved the harsh winters in the upper peninsula of Michigan, and spent my teen years in New Mexico. I have had the great pleasure of experiencing many of the different regional cultures our country has to offer. One of the aspects of the internal national cultures was that, even within our borders, those separate national cultures differed from region to region.

Not only did I have the opportunity to see and experience these differences with my own eyes, I myself am of a mixed race. My dad is of Irish descent, and my mother is Mexican. So I was viewing the national cultures from two different cultures of my own, and my greatest observation was this; not only are Mexicans different from Americans, they are different from Mexicans from another region in the U.S. New Mexico has its very own Mexican culture different from all others, including Mexico itself. The Mexican in New Mexico dresses differently than the Mexican in Arizona, just one state away. How could this be? If immigration laws stifle the growth of other nation's cultures, how do these cultures continue to grow and develop in our country? The answer is: they couldn't if immigration laws truly were enacted to prevent multicultural development.

Many Americans question the reasoning behind limiting a particular nationality over another or why we would use immigration laws to prevent the underprivileged from entering our country when that previously mentioned quote is written so plainly on the Statue of Liberty. The argument being, laws of this nature are racist and do nothing but stifle our multicultural identity. It is true that through the modern era of immigration (from 1952 onward) our laws had prevented and accommodated different nationalities based on our own country's needs. What also needs to be addressed is: At times our leaders understood the need to increase immigration to protect those in need. We need to tell the whole story of immigration, not just the side that supports a particular stance on a given political ideology.

The Immigration and Nationality Act (INA) of 1952, which was signed into law by President Truman, established the fundamentals of our current immigration standards. Its major premise was derived from the fears of Soviet infiltration and communist assimilation into the American ideology. It also kept the quota system from the Naturalization Act of 1790 while adding the preference system based on nationality and labor market demands. Then, in 1965, President Johnson –another Democrat– signed the INA of 1965. This provided for country specific quotas. Again, the job market would have more say in what countries and how long an immigrant could stay. This is an example of Big Government using big business to control immigration and cultural influence in our country. The sweeping change in immigration came in 1986 when President Reagan signed the Immigration Reform and Control Act of 1986.

This would be the first major legislation on immigration to address sanctions for companies which were hiring illegal immigrants. It also provided amnesty for those already in the U.S. and were paying taxes and assimilating into the American way of life. However, this bill fell short of addressing the effects on illegal immigration amongst juveniles. President Reagan opted to use his executive powers to account for children and provide amnesty for anyone under the age of eighteen. All subsequent attempts at immigration reform have been largely procedural, yet the major tenant of each Immigration Reform Act is the support to American Companies. So, with American business being the primary focus of immigration reform since 1965, what is the overall net effect to the economy for a cultural perspective? In short, it has actually created greater discrimination within the job market.

I will concede that this is primarily in day labor, farming and technology industries, so it is not in the greater expanse of U.S. industries as a whole. But, from a fundamental and moral standpoint, having the economy as our focus for immigration has actually caused the cultural discrimination the American people have been screaming about in the first place, allowing companies to show preferential hiring pairing skill to labor at a reduced cost all while using the effects of national inflation to inflate prices while keeping costs down. If multicultural protection should not be the focus, and an economic focus on immigration actually has a negative effect on multiculturalism, what should be the primary focus of our immigration laws? In a word: Nationalism.

Nationalism actually protects both the economy and multiculturalism because it demands the immigrant assimilate to the American ideal while allowing individuals to express their national culture. The individual even has the ability to then express his or her culture from a regional perspective by assimilating to the local culture of the new residence. This aspect of immigration assimilation is commonplace in the modern military family, and I don't just mean the husband, wife, and child nuclear family. I am referring to the extended family all military service members belong to. Many of the men and women I have served with over the course of my twenty-five year career have had spouses from other countries. Every time I went to a different friend's house it was like walking into a different country. The smells in any given home would be representative of the culture of the foreign born spouse. While I never asked any service members why they defaulted to the spouse's culture in their home, I did make a bold assumption. That assumption is that they understood the need for their spouses to have a bit of home with them in a foreign land. Yet, the spouses were required to assimilate to the American ideal. They were not allowed to drive on the left side of the road. They were required to enroll in the Defense Enrollment Eligibility System (DEERS), show proof of authorization of access to the installation in which they lived, as well as many other aspects of military life they had to adjust to. Failure to do so would have meant they would no longer be allowed to enjoy the benefits of the system. This is just a small example of the importance of nationalism as the foundation for our immigration laws.

There is also a much deeper reason to establish nationalism as the moral foundation of our laws: It is to protect the American way of life from corrupt foreign influences. I would like to share two very real-world examples of how the corruption of national identity has led to the downfall of one nation and the rise of a tyrant in another. The latter will show how the tyrant had the foresight to see the true effects of immigration to spread his communist ideology across generations. With Vladimir Lenin taking control of the Russian Empire after the October Rebellion of 1917, the principles of communism took root in Eastern Europe and Northeast Asia. It is what Lenin did between 1922 and 1924 that would affect the newly formed Soviet Union and even modern day Russia.

Lenin was truly in it for the long game. He had an understanding and the patience to see the long-term effects of his nation-building of communist doctrine. In 1922 Lenin began to implement a plan to utilize immigration laws to affect Russian presence in all of the Soviet countries, and it was pure genius. He relocated families living in impoverished and desolate areas in Russia to more fertile areas of the newly acquired countries that made up the Soviet Union. He also granted dual citizenship for those transplanted Russian nationals. This allowed for citizens of Russia to then vote in the government elections of their new communities.

The risk Lenin took was that the transplanted Russians would remain loyal to Russian culture and vote in favor of Russian/communist ideals in these other countries. After all, it was Lenin who moved them from the harsh environments and economic poverty to much more fertile and economically prosperous countries. While the intended effect was not immediately felt, a transformation had begun. It was the younger generations who began to spread communist ideology throughout the Soviet Union, the effect of which is still felt today. One need only look to the Russian annexation of Crimea in March of 2014.

On 22 February 2014, the Russian President, Vladimir Putin, was able to use Russian nationals within the Crimean Peninsula to execute pro-Russian demonstrations in order to exacerbate an already unstable region of the Ukraine–which was caused by the ousting of Ukrainian President, Viktor Yanukovych. The pro-Russian protesters then voted against the Crimean Parliament and its support of the newly established government in Kiev. They also established civil defense forces in support of Russian military involvement in easing the unrest in the peninsula. The mounting pressure from the pro-Russian nationals led to the election of a Russian mayor of Sevastopol. This crisis in national identity opened the door to military occupation on February 27, 2014, at which time the Russian military blocked access to the Supreme Council of Crimea building.

Now Russia has its sights set on the Baltic Region. President Putin has a desire to see the Soviet Union restored to the glory days of the Cold War. He has increased Russian military presence near the Baltic region and has increased military training exercises as well. This has invoked a response from NATO by increasing a military presence and conducting multinational training exercises led by the U.S. Army. The question that needs to be asked at this point is would Putin risk an invasion into the Baltics knowing these actions would invoke a military response from NATO? No, he would not. With the large Russian population that resides in the Baltics he has a different game plan, the same plan exercised in Crimea. He will allow for civil action to take place in the region and use Russian nationals already inside the country's borders to vote in favor of Russian ideology. It is not the fastest path to victory, but it has proven to be a very successful formula.

Russian leaders are not the only ones to use National ideology to take control of a region of another country. So who was another other leader to employ such a tactic? Yep, you guessed it, Adolf Hitler. The difference here is that he actually used the entire European leadership to sign legal documentation agreeing to use occupation of another country. With the occupation of the Sudetenland, we see again how civil unrest within the country of Czechoslovakia allowed for Nazi Germany to use national identity to influence an unarmed occupation of a nation.

As I look across the American political spectrum I hear statements from the Left like [9]"we are in this for the long-haul." I see the desires of many Americans to

---

[9] *Inside Elizabeth Warren's grassroots strategy*, MJ Lee, 15 March 2019

overlook immigration laws they view as racist. This has established sanctuary cities in which individuals, who have not assimilated into the American culture, are given voting rights to influence leadership decisions within our borders. This screams of the communist and socialist examples given above of how immigration is used to weaken national will and allow foreign influence to topple a government without ever having to invade with militarily force. Also, I see the purposeful unrest the media perpetuates throughout the daily news cycle, inciting its people to pick one side or the other and then screaming how evil you are to have not selected the side they told you to select. Both sides use this tactic to preach their brand of politics to an ever agitated population.

    The greatest threat to our national ideals is the failure to ensure assimilation of our immigrants into the American way of life. Nationalism as the foundation for our immigration actually encourages economic growth and enhances multiculturalism, not just as the nation at large, but even throughout specific geographical regions within the United States. It does so by ensuring every individual who enters our borders legally knows what it means to be an American and understands how our laws are meant to encourage citizens to fairly compete on the open job market, free of discrimination, and to choose their representation at all levels of government while ensuring the elected officials answer to a system of checks and balances to prevent the government from becoming tyrannical. Failing to establish proper immigration laws that protect these ideals will ensure they do not survive.

4

"Book 'em, Danno"

> "If possible, as much as lieth in you, live peaceably with all men... Avenge not yourselves, vengeance in mine... saith the Lord...Be not overcome of evil., but overcome evil with good."
>
> Romans 12: 18 – 21

As we address the issues surrounding crime and punishment in the United States, we, as a society, must stipulate that there will always be individuals who commit crimes. This stipulation must form the foundation for the formation of all laws, procedures, punitive measures and rehabilitative efforts. A realistic understanding of human behavior is required in order to develop a realistic outcome of decreasing overall crime in this country. To believe that the creation of more laws criminalizing certain behaviors will result in the reduction of crime is to ignore the fact that it is criminals who break the laws in the first place. We have reached a legal saturation point with the number of laws on our books in most states.

A three strike rule or some variation of it is enforced by many states. All this has done is ensure that those continuously committing crimes will do more time for subsequent violations. Criminals often wind up receiving longer sentences for lesser crimes, such as a parole violation for missing curfew. The result of this legislative mindset has led to overcrowded prisons and an increase in recidivism rates. The overcrowding issue leads to the release of prisoners who are more apt to be repeat offenders, resulting in greater crimes committed against our law abiding citizens.

Verses one and two of Romans chapter twelve tell us that the only way to see change develop is by renewing our minds. We will not see a reduction in crime if we do not renew the way in which we see the criminal, primarily focusing on the reintegration of the offender once his or her debt to society has been paid. The way we have been viewing this problem is strictly from a standpoint of prevention. "Take the drugs off the street and the dealers will go away." "Remove the dealers and the drugs go away." None of this is true. Removing a particular drug or the dealer simply creates a vacuum in which another faux pharmaceutical distributor rises up in order to fill the void, often with more lethality than the previous one.

This is not to say that there should not be a focus on crime prevention because that is certainly a need. After all, a civilized society must have well established boundaries of acceptable behavior that are also well defined. Moreover, there must be a way of punishing those who choose to live outside of those boundaries. There must also be an established way to reintroduce those individuals whom we, as a society, have deemed fit to rejoin our communities once their punishment is complete. Lawmakers and criminal institutions have simply ignored this aspect of the judicial process.

Instead, conservatives have opted for harsher sentences and longer prison terms to reduce criminal behavior, the prevailing wisdom relying more on deterrence to scare the criminal into upright conduct. The left simply blames society for much of the criminal activity. They state that since society and its laws have created an environment in which criminals are created, they should not be held accountable for their criminal exploits. This often results in light sentences and an increase in recidivism rates. Again, both sides lack compassion for the individuals caught in the criminal justice system. The Right fails to see the need for true rehabilitation to assist with reintegration. The Left fails to care for the communities it is supposed to protect.

The primary focus for true reduction in crime must be achieved by reducing recidivism rates through desistance. According to The Oxford English Dictionary, recidivism is simply the tendency for a criminal to reoffend, whether it is a greater or lesser offense, and desistance is the cessation from criminal or other antisocial behavior. Many criminals, who are incarcerated, whether in the juvenile, local, state, or federal facilities, will breathe free air again. According to sentenceproject.org, approximately 89% of all inmates doing time will be paroled in their lifetime. The remaining 11% are those who have been sentenced to "life without parole" or been given a sentence in which it is deemed improbable the inmate will survive to complete his or her sentence. Our communities should be very concerned with the way in which these criminals are rehabilitated while in the care of the criminal justice system because how they come out is going to determine how they act as new members of our communities. Are our elected officials ensuring those offenders are reentering our communities truly rehabilitated and ready to start a new life? I do not believe they are.

The Department of Justice (DOJ) released a report in April, 2014 concerning recidivism rates in the United States. The study gathered information on prisoners released in 2005 from over thirty States and focused on four main categories: Violent Crimes, Property, Drug Related Offenses, and Public Order. Crimes, such as parole violations, weapons related charges not associated with violent crimes, and Driving Under the Influence (DUI) fell under the Public Order category. [10]Violent crimes accounted for 27.4% of all crimes committed by inmates released in 2005. With property at 29.1%, drug offenses accounted for 31.4% and public order with 12.1%. The report then looked at the rearrest rate of all the inmates released in 2005 over the next five years. The average recidivism rate was 43% within the first year across all four categories. That number rose to 76% of all criminals released being rearrested within five years of being released.

These statistics tell the story of a society that is not producing many new criminals. We are simply recycling the majority of criminals which are in our communities. These criminals continue to prey on the law abiding citizens, which are trusting law makers to enact legislation to prevent this very thing. Yet, they have not done their part. As I mentioned early on in this chapter, it is going to

---

[10] Durose, Matthew R., Alexia D. Cooper, and Howard N. Snyder, *Recidivism of Prisoners Released in 30 States in 2005: Patterns from 2005 to 2010*, Bureau of Justice Statistics Special Report, April 2014, NCJ 244205.

take a renewing of our minds in order to understand the true changes needed in our society if we want to see a decrease in repeat offenders. To see the number of repeat offenders drop is to truly impact the negative crime statistic.

Another important factor to consider is the effectiveness of probation and supervised parole on recidivism. There is no shortage of information on this topic. Several studies have been conducted, with varying results. The results run the spectrum from not very effective to very effective as long as strict parameters are followed. These parameters are: [11]probation/parole officer skill level, pro-social modeling and reinforcement, problem solving, the use of cognitive techniques, worker-client relationship, risk levels of clients, and other factors. All of the reports draw a consistent conclusion: Supervised parole alone has no effect on reducing recidivism rates, regardless of the type of crime committed. Conversely, supervised parole coupled with sound treatment has a lesser chance of the criminal reoffending.

I am not advocating for the end of the supervised parole program nor a reduction in the crime prevention efforts of law enforcement agencies. However, I do believe there is a critical component missing in the true effectiveness of reducing crime in our country. It has to do with the incarceration component to the criminal justice system. This issue is not tied to shorter or lesser sentences for a given crime but rather the method by which criminals are incarcerated at large and the treatment, care, and punitive

---

[11] Chris TrotterMonash University, Australia, *Reducing Recidivism Through Probation Supervision: What We Know and Don't Know From Four Decades of Research,* September 2013.

measures taken to assist the offender with reintegration and desistance from criminal behavior.

The first aspect of the incarceration process that must be looked at is how and where a criminal is housed while in jail or prison. Often, criminals who have committed non-violent crimes are housed with violent offenders. So a white-collar criminal who took advantage of the elderly is now living with a person who might have committed murder. Now the non-violent offender has to "toughen up" in order to survive the harsh conditions of an unforgiving and hostile environment. The result is an individual who went in to pay for his or her crime of a non-violent nature returning to society with a harsher disposition and a lack of empathy for a world that does not seem to care for the experiences he or she was exposed to while incarcerated.

In order to help reduce repeat offenders, lawmakers must secondly reconsider the practice of housing parolee potential inmates with inmates serving life sentences. An individual who has been given a life sentence knows his or her fate and, as a result, has a different world view. These individuals have no hope of release. Allowing them to then influence the emotional disposition of a person who has the ability to rejoin society is, at best, reckless. An inmate is already fighting an uphill battle in just hoping for parole in the first place. Compounding that struggle with the constant bombardment of negative, and often violent, behavior leaves no wonder as to why we see such recidivism rates in the U.S.

The third aspect to be considered is treatment. Every criminal who commits a crime usually falls within particular psychological spectrums. Murderers tend to fall into one particular spectrum while bank robbers fall into another. Gang members fall into one, rapists in another, and so forth. Treatment focused on the individual and the crime committed has been shown to reduce repeat offenses in parolees. Therefore, it stands to reason that providing mandatory treatment prior to parole would result in even greater reduction in repeat offenders returning to prison. Moreover, society as a whole would be a much safer place to live.

So, the question is: Are there any examples from which we can draw to see if the above mentioned processes have been successful? Yes, in the laws we have criminalizing sex offenses and the way we treat and release sex offenders to rejoin our society. [12]In 1985, a rehabilitation counselor, Robert Longo, concluded in an article written for *Psychology Today* that "80% of all sex offenders would reoffend if they did not receive proper treatment". However, more recent studies have concluded that the repeat offense rates for sex offenders are between 5% and 7%. What caused such a drastic drop in sex crime recidivism rates? There are many factors leading to successful reductions in such crimes.

The first factor was fear and misunderstanding. The above mentioned reference from Robert Longo led to a ruling by Justice Anthony Kennedy in which he made the statement that the potential for a sex offender to re-offend was *"frightening and high."* At the time of the ruling in 1994, there was no empirical data to support the claim that the recidivism of sex crimes was that high. However, what ensued from this ruling eventually paved the way for a huge reduction in sex crimes throughout society.

---

[12] Steven Yoder, Pacific Standard Staff, *What's the Real Rate of Sex-Crime Recidivism,* 14 June 2017

The fear and misunderstanding then led to lawmakers enacting laws to bring about real change in reducing sex crime re-offense. The first step was adding sex offenders to a national registry. This is in line with supervised parole. Individuals who commit sex crimes now have to register with local law enforcement and are placed on a national registry which provides communities with the residence and workplaces of individuals who have committed sex crimes. They are watched heavily by both law enforcement and local communities. As a personal note, my wife and I check the national registry on a regular basis to stay informed about the community in which we raise our children.

The one true, great success that came from the Longo study and subsequent Yoder article was the need for treatment focused on the specific behavior of the offender. A rapist is different from a child sex offender, and child sex offenders also differ from one other based on victimology. Having a system in place while the offender is in custody and treating the specific behavior of the individual is crucial for successfully ensuring desistance by sex offenders.

The fourth factor was merely a byproduct of the Department of Correction's (DOC) mandate to ensure safe housing for individuals incarcerated in any detention facility, jail, or prison in the U.S. Years ago, when sex offenders were sent to jail, they were simply placed into general population. This caused many inmates to commit acts of violence against sex offenders. Since the DOC was required by law to keep inmates safe, they were placed in separation cells and isolated from everyone else, or they were placed in areas of the prison designated for sex offenders. This separated them from individuals who would not only do them physical harm but could negatively influence their world view. They were now free from the "fight or flight" stressors the majority of other inmates suffer at the hands of more aggressive and violent inmates.

With the evidence of a success pattern to reducing recidivism in criminal behavior being seen, one has to wonder why law makers are not implementing the aforementioned changes. It would be easy to say it is a budget issue, which I believe is the "easy button" we allow law makers to use in order to forego truly fixing the issues we have with crime and punishment in our country. The greatest inhibitor to seeing real change is not altering the way we view criminals in our society. We see them as sinners who are unredeemable and undeserving a second chance, even after they pay their debts to society.

Another factor related to reducing recidivism– though not tied to the incarceration process but worth mentioning–is self-identification. This is the idea that once a criminal has paid his debt, he is forgiven of his crime and able to move on with his life and make a fresh start. Many criminals who have been paroled find it difficult to reintegrate back into society due to the stigma that comes with being a former convict. This leads to unemployment and failed relationships. This, in turn, leads to feeling like a failure unable to care for one's self. Many former convicts thus default to the life they have become accustomed to and resort to criminal behavior.

The federal government has offered several incentive programs to assist with the hiring of people with disabilities, people working in under-resourced yet critical jobs, as well as veterans. As a veteran, I was given several opportunities to attend trades schools while still on active duty. That means I would have been receiving all of my pay and entitlements as an active duty soldier but would be given the time off work to attend a trade school. All of this was in preparation for my transition out of the Army. I was also given a list of companies who have preferential hiring for veterans.

The same resources that I was given in order to make my transition out of the military easier could also be given to assist former inmates with living a "henceforth life." In II Corinthians 5:15-16 we are challenged to live a "henceforth life" after we seek forgiveness from God. That means, once I am granted forgiveness by God, the sin I committed is no longer held against me. So should it be with the way we treat those whom we have said have committed a crime but paid their debt to society. I would have no issue with companies that provide jobs for former inmates receiving subsidies in order to help former inmates get back on their feet.

We need to see the value in ensuring that those who have committed crimes against us can rejoin society as productive members. We need to elect officials who will work to enact legislation that will ensure a true reduction in crime, not simply criminalize behavior with more laws. It is going to take a leader in the Department of Justice with the courage to ignore party politics and develop procedures based on the findings of the above mentioned reports as well as an analysis of those reports in order to see quantifiable changes to criminal behavior in our country.

5

DEPARTMENT OF DEFENSE?

"The horse is prepared against the day of battle: but safety is of the Lord."

Proverbs 21: 31

In a post 9/11 world, the military has seen a resurgence of patriotic support reminiscent of the 1940s. This is in stark contrast to the feelings of society at large for the military during the Vietnam conflict. My father would regale us with stories of his friends returning home from Vietnam only to get spit on or have a drink poured on them while in an airport or boarding a plane. One such story goes: A friend of his, heading home, was boarding a plane in Seattle, WA while wearing his military uniform. As he passed through the first class cabin, a woman stood up and spit in his face. This woman happened to be a professional golfer with the LPGA. I can't even imagine what it must have felt like to have come home from such a brutal conflict only to be spit on by your own countrymen.

Fast forward to 2019, and the patriotic landscape looks tremendously different. If anyone says anything critical of the military, they risk being labeled unpatriotic or un-American, as if asking our military leadership to evaluate its successes and failures in order to improve as an organization is somehow unpatriotic. Quite to the contrary, asking any of our nation's leaders to constantly reevaluate an organization's processes to determine the best way to ensure success is a very pro-American concept. In this chapter I will take a critical look at the military and provide some recommendations as a way-ahead for its future. But, before I get too critical of the military, I would like to take some time to share how it has affected my life for the better.

I joined the New Mexico Army National Guard in August of 1992 during the summer between my junior and senior years of high school. As a senior attending Cibola high school in Albuquerque, I was a starting wrestler at 125lbs and spending one weekend a month with Bravo Battery, 7th Battalion/200th Air Defense Artillery in Rio Rancho. My military career would eventually lead to serving in the Colorado National Guard, the U.S. Navy, and completing my career with the U.S. Army. I entered the service as a Private Second Class and retired as a Chief Warrant Officer Four in the Field Artillery. I have done everything from cleaning toilets to briefing the Army Chief of Staff on digital compatibility of U.S. fire support systems and NATO nations' digital support architecture.

I was the Deputy Director for Targeting for all of Afghanistan. I was the lead Fire Support Planner for the initial planning stages of the Regionally Aligned Forces Mission Command Element in Europe, and I conducted joint planning and training sessions with many NATO partnered nations. I have been abased and I have abounded. So, how does a kid from the small town of Rio Rancho, NM (a place I am sure many of you reading this have never even heard of) become someone who helped influence the military infrastructure at a strategic level?

I would like to say it was an easy journey, but I would be lying. However, what it required was simple. I dedicated my efforts to honing my craft as a warrior. I know it's not popular to talk like this today, but it is what was required. I applied the principles and tenants of combat and leadership as well as developed attributes the military determined would make me a successful and mature leader. The military taught and trained me to be the man I am today: a mature, out-of-the-box, deliberate thinker who never identifies a problem without also developing viable solutions. Sadly, I believe the modern military as has abandoned many of these principles and tenants, to its own failure. This is why an honest critique of our military is both timely and necessary.

The greatest problem plaguing the American military today is a lack of a clearly stated "end state" for our presence in the majority of theaters in which U.S. personnel are currently deployed. There has been an inside joke floating around many military staff planning teams for quite some time. "We are all velocity and no vector." The sentiment highlights the fact that military planners are very busy and work long hours, only to have to continue the processes over and over again each day. Much like the movie *Groundhog's Day,* military planners live the same day over and over again without any change in the outcome. Their efforts are in vain because they are not achieving victory.

On October 7, 2001 the U.S. military invasion of Afghanistan began. At the beginning, the U.S. military had clear and concise goals: Find Osama Bin Laden, bring him to justice, remove the Taliban from power, and deny them freedom to conduct terrorist activities within the country. Once the initial invasion was complete and military advisory determined finding Bin Laden would take longer than expected, the focus shifted from the above stated, clearly defined goals, to the less achievable goal of ridding the country of all terrorists and any terrorist associated activities. To sum up this end state, the goal became to fixing everything wrong with Afghanistan. This established an unrealistic measure of success by any standard.

We cannot fix everything that is wrong in our own country. What makes us think we have the ability to fix thousands of years of governing and warring ideologies in another nation? The answer is simple: we cannot. A military end state philosophy such as this one is like saying the only way a football team can declare victory is to keep the other team scoreless throughout the competition. According to NFL.com, only 3.8% of all National Football League games end with one team being shutout. Once both teams score, neither team can be declared the victor. This is exactly what is happening in Afghanistan right now. The military leaders state that since terrorist attacks are still being conducted, we still have reason to continue the conflict. Well, let us apply the same metric to the United States.

Since we have so many illegal immigrants from Mexico committing crimes in the U.S., does the Mexican government then get a say in whether they should be involved in our defense? Of course the answer is no. So why do our military and political leaders think the only measure of success in Afghanistan is the total elimination of all terrorist activity? I will be honest with you; I do not have an answer for the why. I can spend a great deal of time speculating, but that is exactly what it would be: speculation. However, due to my time spent overseas participating in the wars in both Iraq and Afghanistan–six combat deployments in all–I can provide a recommendation for what should define success in the region.

Complete desistance from all terrorist activity, or even the reduction of terrorist activity by any measurable percentage, is a failing means for defining success. The only measure of defining success in Afghanistan is through tribal affiliation. This is not to say that the U.S. picks its favorite tribe and supports its rise to power by ensuring that tribal leadership rules at a federal level. Rather, it is an understanding of which tribe will bring peace and stability in any given geographical region within the country. With the Afghanistan military and political leaders in the lead, having them establish the principles of mediation between warring tribes builds the trust and confidence of the Afghan people in their own government.

This is how they have governed themselves for thousands of years. It is a bit ambitious for the U.S. to assume it can change thousands of years of ideology in just a few decades. Afghanistan is a sovereign nation and deserves to be recognized as such and allowed to govern itself the way it sees fit. It certainly is not the right of America to fix Afghanistan, either. Unless we as a country agree that Mexico should be allowed to send troops to help us curb our immigration problem (go back and read chapter 3 if you think they should be allowed), then we need to develop a sound exit strategy from Afghanistan. I know many of you reading this book might be saying,

DEPARTMENT OF DEFENSE?

"Alright, mister smarty pants, what does an exit strategy from Afghanistan look like?" I am glad you asked.

Operation Sovereignty will be a four-phased operation. Phase I will begin with the publication of the Afghanistan government's developed principles of mediation and ends with Afghan political and military leaders conducting negotiations with warring tribes. Phase II begins with the U.S. leading combat operations in order to destroy known terrorist activity staging areas, and manufacturing facilities. This phase ends with the Afghanistan military leading reconstruction efforts. Phase III is Afghanistan only combat operations and initial withdrawal of U.S. military. This is a time based phase and ends at the one year mark of the initial start of Operation Sovereignty. Phase IV is the final phase and is the transfer of responsibility and final withdrawal of U.S. military personnel from Afghanistan. The only remaining U.S. troop presence at the end of this operation is those personnel providing protection for the U.S. embassy in Kabul.

The breakdown of each phase will look something like the following: The governance phase will last approximately three months. While it will not be a time-based phase, placing a timeline on each phase will be vitally important to ensuring that the progression through each phase has a sense of urgency. The focus of this phase will be on governance and information operations. Both Afghan and U.S. News outlets will broadcast that the Afghan government is developing the plan to allow for U.S. military withdrawal over the next eighteen months. The following is what the narrative should look like and will be the prevailing narrative throughout the entire operation:

"An assessment of the future of Afghanistan as a sovereign and self-governing nation is being conducted. Over the next few weeks the Afghanistan government will be developing the principles of tribal mediation with the goal of bringing peace to the wonderful people of Afghanistan."

U.S. military leadership's involvement during this phase will be virtually non-existent. This phase must be led entirely by Afghan leadership in order to ensure acceptance from the people of Afghanistan. The U.S. State Department's involvement will be limited to a role as a historical witness as well as providing updates to U.S. administration and military leadership. This will ensure adherence to the urgency requirements to continue making progress and moving forward with the operation. The greatest challenge during this phase will be overcoming bureaucratic road blocks that tend to impede progress.

Phase II will be when the U.S. military leads combat operations throughout the entire country. The focus will be to conduct deliberate strikes against known terrorist locations. The primary reason for this is to disrupt terrorist activities throughout the country. The secondary reason for the U.S. leading these attacks is that it will facilitate the Afghanistan army's legitimacy for affecting reconstruction efforts during this phase while simultaneously affecting delays in terrorist activity. The Afghanistan political leaders will simultaneously be conducting desistance efforts though tribal mediation. The anticipated timeline for these events will be approximately six months.

With the Afghanistan leadership established as the lead facilitators for their own country's governance and military defense, the Phase III timeline is anticipated as lasting only three months. This phase is when Afghanistan begins conducting unilateral operations and U.S. military personnel begin their withdrawal from Afghanistan. This withdrawal will begin in areas experiencing the greatest reduction in terrorist activity. If there are regions of very little conflict prior to Operation Sovereignty beginning, wisdom dictates withdrawal beginning there first.

Phase IV, the final phase of the operation, is when the U.S. Military will begin transferring all facilities, closing out any debts to Afghanistan (i.e. Internet, electricity, fuel, food), and sharing appropriate level intelligence information and any other information deemed vital to the successful transfer of responsibility to the Afghanistan military. With six months remaining in Operation Sovereignty, the Resolute Support (RS) commander will determine the sequence of closure for units operating in each of the remaining Train, Advise, Assist Commands (TAAC) with the RS headquarters in Kabul being the last command to withdraw at the end of the eighteenth month.

There will clearly be greater requirements as well as specified and implied tasks needed to complete Operation Sovereignty. This does, however, provide an excellent framework to establish a withdrawal timeline from Afghanistan by defining what true success looks like in that theater of operations. Our political and military leadership owes it to the American public to define success in Afghanistan and determine the method of withdrawal. We are the ones investing our sons and daughters into this conflict. We should be demanding this answer as well. My hope is that this chapter will gather the attention of the American people and inspire our nation's leaders to action and end this protracted war that is costing American service members' lives.

Another aspect in which presidential administrations do a huge disservice to the military is in using it as a means of pushing social change on society at large. I have heard it said by several leaders throughout my time in the military in both the Navy and Army, that the military should be a direct reflection of American society at large. If this idea is to be successful then the military will not be. In turn, if the military is to be successful then this idea can never be fully implemented. The first example I will give in combating this is that every branch of service does one thing when a recruit first arrives at basic training/boot camp. They take away the individual's identity to his or her society by cutting his or her hair. This is done to strip away the foundation of the recruit's individuality. American society says it is my individuality that makes my contribution to society more unique and valuable. The military says a soldier's individuality is only as important as needed to accomplish the mission. Individual human expression is subverted for the sake of the unit. This philosophy from the outset is a violation of a societal law as well as the military.

Another reason why the military is a poor avenue to determine the success of social change is that military personnel can be forced to comply. So, an organization established not to accept change but be forced to comply is not exactly a great metric to determine the accuracy of American society at large. At its core, the U.S. military is a dictatorship. Soldiers can take recourse if they feel any leader's behavior is in violation of basic individual rights. But, there again, the military has a different understanding of what human rights are. And it must be this way. Why? It must be this way because we are asking service members to go to other nations and kill other people. I know it is not popular to talk this way, violently and harshly, but the harsh reality is that no other industry in American society says their company is designed to kill people for a living. Thus, the requirements for its people are going to be completely different.

I am not saying the military can never be used to help society understand its ability to accept social change; rather that it should not be used as the only means of forcing social change. There is only one aspect that should be considered when using the military as a social experiment, and that is readiness. Any other factors being considered for social engineering of our military is to weaken the function of what the military does: win wars and armed conflict by defeating its enemies on the battlefield. If any aspect of social engineering reduces America's ability to deploy, fight, and win, it is a failure. With all that said, now let's talk about the two most talked about social engineering topics in our military today: women in combat and transgender soldiers.

Should women be allowed in combat? My answer is yes, but how will it affect readiness? That is a very good question. The biggest way is pregnancy. A woman is not allowed to deploy when she is pregnant. If an infantry unit is thirty percent female (the same percentage of women who serve in non-combat arms units, such as a support battalion), and fifty percent of them get pregnant within three months of a deployment, the unit will deploy below strength. This places the remaining soldiers at greater risk. They will be on combat patrols with less combat power during any given engagement. This is an unacceptable risk to ask our service members to accept.

So how do we reduce that risk? Once a unit is identified for a combat deployment, the females in that unit must comply with a contraception regimen that will ensure they will not get pregnant. We then get into the discussion of a woman's reproductive rights if we are to keep with an accurate reflection of American society at large. And to consider those rights is to endanger the majority of any given combat unit. So, again, by the shear nature of what the military does, it can never be an accurate reflection of American society but can be used to allow for acceptance, as long as readiness is not compromised.

The transgender topic has a few more layers to it, but the issue is already fifty percent solved. Before I get to how that is so, I would like to discuss the layers that must be solved. The first question to ask is: should transgender individuals be allowed to serve in the military? Yes, provided any aspect of their transition does not affect readiness. Now we must identify ways in which a transitioning soldier will affect readiness, which is simple enough to accomplish. Any surgeries, psychological treatments, and recovery needed to complete their transition must not take place while on active duty or in such a manner as to reduce the combat readiness of any given unit. A soldier may not use the Permanent Change of Station (PCS) protocol to take advantage of a unit's readiness cycle. In other words, transitioning soldiers would not be allowed to petition their branch manager/detailer to move to another unit that is not deploying in order to complete their transition when their current unit has been placed on deployment status.

If individuals are biologically male but identify as female and apply for entry in the military as females, they will be required to attend basic training/boot camp as their biologically assigned sex. If they have male reproductive organs, they will be assigned to male barracks/berths. Here is where I will be met with the argument that I am a nasty, mean, bigot who does not care about transgender rights. I will redirect people who make this argument to my previous statements concerning the military's first step of any recruit, which is to take away individuality for the sake of the unit. So, again, this forced social engineering is in violation of American society at large as well as the military's need to lose individual identity over the need for team unity.

As transgender soldiers are required to live in the quarters of their biologically assigned genders, something interesting will occur. At first, they will feel isolated just like every other individual they are going through training with. Every recruit will be thinking the same thing: "My suffering is worse than your suffering." And, they are correct, to a degree. Then, as each individual grows personally, something else will happen. They will come to the realization that everyone is suffering. This will happen at different times for different people. Those individuals who learn it sooner will then begin to help those who are still learning. Then, something absolutely spectacular will take place; they will grow into a team, a team that cares for one another, a team that will cheer for one another. Why does this happen? It is because of a concept of shared experiences. Those who suffer together have no choice but to grow together. This is a guarantee.

So, when do transgender Soldiers get to feel like they are part of the team while getting to express themselves with some semblance of individuality? That happens when they get to their first duty station and beyond. Here is a scenario to help explain this concept. The transgender Soldier arrives at their first command, and in their enlistment paperwork it states the individual has a personal identity different from the biological gender. The soldier will be placed in quarters relative to their biological gender until a full transition can be made. The soldier, seeing the unit is not slated for a deployment, begins transition procedures. They begin transition procedures and use personal leave time for recovery. They must use leave time because it is an elective surgery and does not require military resources to allow for recovery time.

Now comes the first step in the military accepting the transition. Once the augmentation is complete and the soldier returns to duty, they will wear the uniform that conforms to the displayed gender. That means if they are female to male and have had a double mastectomy, they will wear the male uniform. If the soldier had implants, then they will wear the female uniform. This will be both for battle fatigues and dress uniform. They will still be required to maintain the quarters of their biological gender. This relationship between the military and the service member will serve to increase trust and confidence that each party involved has the other's best interest in mind while keeping the unit ready to deploy at full strength.

I mentioned previously that the military has already solved fifty percent of the transgender argument. I am going to share two personal stories to illustrate how this is true. When I joined the military, I was a virgin. This caused many an uncomfortable moment for me in my training as well as a certain level of ridicule when I arrived at my unit. Through all of the ridicule, I never claimed to be a victim. I simply took the jokes and sent some trash talk back in the direction of my tormentors. We laughed and developed into a pretty well-oiled crew. Again, our shared experiences in the hot New Mexico summer sun developed in us a bond of misery.

Let's fast forward to my first Roving Sands training event at White Sands Missile Range in Southern New Mexico. We had one sleep tent for the entire battery, minus the battery commander and first sergeant. So, for the first time in my life I was sleeping in the same room as a woman. There was one female that was a bit more outgoing than the other. She liked to lie around in just her panties and put her feet up on the tent post. The proud display she had for her figure made me uncomfortable, yet at no time did I feel she did not have the right to serve her country. I went up to her and asked her to put her feet down. She declined, saying she had every right to walk around in her underwear just like all the men did.

In the morning I had a talk with my battery executive officer about the incident. He called her over to our table where we were eating breakfast, and we discussed the issue. I know it must be strange to have three grownups talking and solving a problem together without a major news outlet getting involved, but that is what we did. We all agreed to be as discreet as possible while in the sleep tent. A group of intelligent adults sat down and came up with a solution and through adversity became a closer team. "Say it ain't so, Joe?!!!"

Now fast forward to my final field problem in the Army. We had multiple sleep tents for the entire division headquarters. Each division staff section was given its own tent. Smaller sections with just a few Soldiers were allowed to sleep in other section tents where space was available. Inevitably, this led to females being housed with males. This happened twenty-five years after the scenario at White Sands, and not a single issue has arisen from the bi-gender sleeping quarters. Why did nothing happen? Because we were professional service members trained to truly find strength in the struggle.

Requiring the military to conform to adapted societal norms is detrimental to the military's mission. Furthermore, the military has already made great strides in ensuring any and all individuals who conform to its laws, principles, and procedures are welcome to serve. It is when individuals with ideology inconsistent with the military demand change that the military ceases to be great at what it does. And what it does is so imperative to the success and health of our country that American society must not dictate how it is to be governed.

The third vital change the military must make is to have younger commanders at the two-star level and down. Our current military is being run by men and women who are grandparents. There is nothing wrong with being a grandpa; I hope to be one someday, but I don't want a bunch of grandparents running the military, which requires some aggressive thinking. These are people who, as part of their decision making process, are worried about losing their pensions. The solution to this issue is simple. Once officers complete their company/battery command time, they are assessed on either a command or staff track.

Currently, by the time officers reach a two-star level command, they have only commanded units for about six years. Furthermore, by the time a leader reaches the two-star level he or she is over the age of forty-six. In contrast, during the Revolutionary War the average age of all general officers was thirty-five. The average age rose slightly by the time the Civil War began to an average age of forty-two. WWI saw that number rise to forty-six. However, this number may be a little misleading due to the fact that the War Department had to reinstate lieutenant generals and generals due to manning issues brought on by the war, many of the lower ranking major and brigadier general ranks being held by men of an average age of forty-five.

WWII and beyond saw the average age of the military general rise to and hold at fifty-two, even to present day. With the exception of WWII, the correlation can easily be made that the older the General Officer Corp, the longer the war lasts. Another correlation is that the older the General Officer Corps, the more political the focus of military leadership becomes. We have an older general officer corps, one that spends only 3.2 percent of its military career actually in command of combat troops, and we wonder why we are struggling to win wars. It might seem like I'm being too critical or even un-American, but the last true commander to win a war for the U.S. was General Norman Schwarzkopf, Jr., who led the U.S. military to victory over the Iraqi Army during the Gulf War in 1991. Let that sink in. 1991 was the last time we had a military commander lead our armed forces to victory.

The best way to eliminate the issues presented above is to develop a two-track officer system. After an officer completes his or her company/battery level command, he or she (average age is 29 years old) is then assessed to either the command or staff track. For the purposes of this discussion, I am only going to follow what the command track will look like. Once the officer is determined to be a command officer, he or she will be promoted to major and spend the next three years as a staff officer in preparation to hold a battalion executive officer (XO) position. After the completion of the third year as a major the officer is promoted to lieutenant colonel and becomes a battalion

XO (32 years old) for the next two years. After completing XO time, the officer becomes the battalion commander (34 years old) for the next two years of the same battalion for which he or she is the executive officer.

After completing time at battalion command, the officer spends one year in charge of a brigade staff section (35 years old). Each brigade has a staff section that represents all war fighting functions across the command. After one year on brigade staff, the officer will be promoted to the rank of colonel and become a brigade XO (36 years old). That position will be held for two years (38 years old), and then the officer becomes that unit's brigade commander (38 years old). Then, at the average age of 40, he or she will be promoted to Brigadier General (BG). The officer's first year as a BG will be spent attending the command and staff college for his or her respective service. The purpose of this course is to focus the leadership on winning large campaign wars. Our current state of modern warfare is clearly campaign in nature, which can be seen by the large number of generals in charge in Afghanistan.

After successful completion of the command and staff college, the officer then becomes a deputy commanding general of a division (40 years old). At this point in the officer's career, there will be more generals than there will be positions. He or she can hold the deputy position for up to five years. Then, if the officer is unable to take division command, he or she is allowed to retire honorably with twenty years of service. After officers successfully assess as division commanders (42 years old), they command a division for a minimum of two years and but no longer than four years. An age restriction of forty-six years old should be placed on the two-star level commands. No leader over the age of forty-six may command a division level command or lower.

Our military leadership needs to be young, fit, and aggressive. It has always been said that good leaders will allow their subordinates the courage to fail. As a warrant officer, I was told to think outside the box, yet every time I demonstrated courage, I was simply told the wrong execution of the right idea. Or, if I thought outside of the box, I was told to get back in the box. This conflicting guidance has become all too real to the modern military service member, who is simply trying to make the military the best fighting force in the world. If you think this statement is incorrect, wait until you hear our military leadership's assessment of this critique.

What was written in this chapter is truly an aggressive approach to solving the modern problems the military faces today. I have applied logic to an out-of-the-box framework that answers many of the public's questions to the protracted war it rarely hears much about anymore. My aim with this chapter was to present both political and military leaders with alternative solutions to the very real problems facing leaders today concerning the future of our military. My hope is that, at the least, this chapter of the book makes it into the hands of senior decision makers within our government and starts a dialogue of focused problem solving to improve the readiness of our department of defense.

6

THE WAR FOR SOCIAL JUSTICE

"Therefore all things whatsoever ye would that men should do to you, do ye even so to them: for this is the law of the prophets."

Matthew 7: 12

The youth of America will soon be the leaders of this great nation. The way in which they are being instructed to govern themselves individually will ultimately determine how they view governance at large. Public and private schools–from primary education to post graduate instruction–have become schools of indoctrination to social conformity as dictated by the predominant liberal agenda in our country's educational system. This prevailing wisdom has resulted in a generation of leaders who believe it is the right and obligation of the government at large to determine and regulate human behavior. Teach the individual to behave in a certain manner, and society will follow. This is a very basic and biblical principle.

Our form of government was founded on this basic principle. The first three words of our constitution state "We the People." This is a clear declaration of where the true foundation of our governing authority comes from: the individual citizens. Even socialist and communist governments understand that it is the will of the people that provides the greatest asset to the success of their ideologies. Change the will of the people, and you will change the way in which they wish to be governed. Convince the people the government knows best then they will vote to have the government make decisions for them. Convince the people themselves that that is the way they wish to be governed. Mussolini convinced the Italian people to forfeit their individual liberties in order to get public transportation in their country to work more efficiently. Change the will of the people, and you can change the course of a country. This is done through indoctrination of ideology. This indoctrination can take place through several different mediums.

Hitler instilled fear as a mechanism for forcing the German people into compliance. This led to neighbor turning on neighbor to avoid any form of reprisal for failure to comply. If you knew your neighbor was making statements against the state and you failed to turn them in, you too could be subject to harsh punishment. Mussolini played on the individual's desire to be cared for. Just forfeit your individual liberties, and we, the state, will provide for all your needs. Here in America, indoctrination happens though our institutions. As discussed in Chapter five, when the president, as commander in chief, wishes to institute a change he or she knows will not pass as a law, he or she mandates the military to conform. Then, through the authority of the commander in chief, the military complies. This is false success. The success of this forced behavioral compliance is due to the fact that military members forfeit many individual rights to serve. So, the American people at large only see the success and say, "Hey, if it works for them, it will work for us," never seeing the fact that the loss of individual liberties is what it took to create that success.

We are seeing this same trend in our educational system. This is where we send our kids to school for up to ten hours a day (if they are involved with extracurricular activities), where they are subject to indoctrination through peer pressure. Comply, or be bullied and shunned. Even if people disagree with the social agenda, if they don't want to be bullied and shunned, they simply keep their mouths shut, and the new standard is established. We have a saying as leaders in the military. "If you ignore a failure to comply with the standard, that behavior then becomes the new standard." This statement is meant to inspire leaders to have the courage to uphold the standards and maintain good order and discipline. This sentiment is echoed in a quote by Edmund Burke: "The only thing necessary for the triumph of evil is for good men to do nothing."

There are two perfect examples of this behavior I experienced in my youth. The first example is when I was in seventh grade science class. I had a registration form for the Young American Football League (YAFL) on my desk in class. While we were conducting a class experiment, one of the popular kids in class saw my registration form. He picked up the form and casually asked me why I had it. I told him I planned on playing football next year. Then, while addressing the class, he began to say there was no way a nerd like me was ever going to play football on his team. Then, two of his friends, also part of the "cool kids" group, began to make fun of me and call me names. One of them actually pushed my head every so often as he made "cry baby" faces at me. It was not long before everyone in the class joined them. Any response I gave was met with the standard "look at spaz, he's gonna cry." After class, some of the students came up to me and expressed their sorrow for the way I was treated, yet they were directly involved in shaming me into not submitting the registration to play football.

The second example happened while riding the bus during my freshman year of high school. There was a group of kids that made it their daily mission to take my homework and throw it out the window of the bus. I had to invent ways to hide my homework in order to keep these kids from stealing it and throwing it away. Wrapping my homework around my legs and tucking it into my socks and tucking it under my shirt and into the waistband of my pants were just some of the ways I hid my homework. Keeping it in my backpack was not an option. They would take my backpack and go through it, looking for my homework and then removing it, crumpling it up, and then laughing at me and making statements like, "Just tell your teacher your dog ate it."

So, on one of the days I was successful in keeping my homework out of the hands of these bullying thieves, they stepped up their game. The bus driver had completed all the stops on her route and we were headed to school. The bullies, a group of four of them, began their routine of taking my backpack and going through it. When they discovered there was no homework, I told them I didn't have any homework from the previous night. One kid suggested I had it in one of my pockets. So they began to take hold of me. That is when everything escalated quickly. I fought back with all my strength. It would prove to fall short of what was needed to repel the attack. They then dragged me to the back of the bus where they proceeded to rip my underwear off of me without having to take off my pants. The result? A torn scrotum and several deep abrasions on my buttocks.

However, the greatest damage was in not having anyone to turn to for help when all this violence was being committed against me. There were at least 30 other kids on that bus, and not one of them had the courage to help. Why? Fear. That is why. Fear they would be caught up in the humiliation and ridicule that was being exercised against me. If they just went along, no harm would come to them. This is the way in which social justice is being indoctrinated into our youth. Comply or suffer as others suffer.

We now have an entire generation of kids growing up in an environment in which certain social behaviors are no longer accepted, and you will bullied and shunned if you do not conform. Harder still is the fact that those doing the bullying and shunning take the stance they are taking the moral high ground. And, just like all under socialist rule, those kids who simply turned a blind eye to the violence against me gave up their personal liberty for the sake of personal safety. The result is a generation of leaders who believe the proper way to rule is through bullied compliance of social normalcy. Well, what they deem as normalcy is based on their interpretation of what morality is to the group, not the individual.

The two dominate, opposing world views concerning the establishment of social justice concepts are from the point of view of the left and the right. The left view is that society (big government) should determine the behavior of the individual. The point of view of the right is that the individual's behavior will determine the success of the society. Both approach their arguments from a point of moral superiority. Each states that the outcome of their arrangement is ultimately for the heart and soul of our country. It is because of this last statement that I believe the concept of social justice is primarily a spiritual concept. Notice that I did not say it is a religious battle. Thus, the battle for the social conscience of America is a spiritual battle. Success on this battleground will not be won by simply claiming the proverbial moral high ground. Rather, it will only be won when we collectively establish the proper moral foundation by which decisions over societal behaviors should be established.

To establish these principles by which our social construct should derive, we must answer two important questions: 1) Does the federal government have the right and/or authority to establish laws regulating social behavior? 2) Should certain social behaviors be criminalized? The answer to the first question is a simple one. No, the federal government does not have the right to regulate social behavior. Our founding fathers knew this and created the Bill of Rights to protect this idea. This is evidence of the founding fathers limiting the power the government has over the governed. The Constitution states that the government derives its power from the consent of the governed. One of the three main compromises of the Constitutional Convention was the establishment of two legislative bodies within the Senate. It was this compromise that established America as a representative republic. However, by way of example, I would like to draw a comparison to this second question.

We already believe as a society that certain behaviors are deemed unworthy of our acceptance, and if people behave contrary to this established behavior, they are separated from society and placed in prison or jail. Both sides of the political aisle concede the fact that we do allow our law makers to create laws for the good of society. If people go around killing people, we call them murderers and throw them in jail. So, as a people in a representative republic, we grant our lawmakers the authority to enact laws on behalf of society. The right side of the political aisle says, "Yes. Just don't mess with the Bill of Rights." The left says, "Hey, I can change any amendment because the constitution is a living, breathing document designed to change as the needs of the country change." And by the way, remember what I discussed in the first few paragraphs of this chapter? Yep, they are the ones establishing the narrative of indoctrination by which future leaders will be voting and making decisions on how we best should be governed.

Going back to the first question: Does the federal government have the right and/or authority to establish laws regulating social behavior? To allow the federal government to regulate human social behavior is to forfeit individual liberty. This loss of individual liberty is fatal to individual dignity. It allows for the state (big government) to determine individual value and worth. There was a time in this country when our government did not value women and would not allow them to vote. African-Americans at one point were not even seen as humans in the eyes of the law. Has history taught us nothing? Why would we go back to a system that allows big government to determine our worth? Furthermore, not only are we moving in that direction as a society at large, we are begging to be governed that way.

How is it possible that we, as a free society of educated thinkers with advanced degrees, would be begging for a system of government which causes us to forfeit the very rights which allowed that system of government into power to begin with? It has happened through the indoctrination processes mentioned previously in this chapter. Currently in our country, our behavior is being regulated not through the rule of law but through bullying and fear of being labeled in a manner inconsistent with the prevailing leftist narrative. The issue will soon be that those currently doing the bullying and shunning will be law makers. Some already are, and they continue to push an agenda that deprives individuals of their personal liberty and, by default, their dignity.

So how does one combat this aggressive indoctrination that has rooted itself in many of the institutions we have entrusted to educate and protect our nation's interests? Is it through an equally aggressive counterattack? Maybe through tolerance and acceptance? Maybe it is just through indifference, the whole "you be you and let me be me mentality." Just let everyone do what they want to do. Both sides of the political aisle know that none of these ideologies are an acceptable way of instituting government rule. As much as the left likes to preach tolerance, it is in no way accepting of Christian principles. Just do a quick search on YouTube for Uber driver fights in California and the "you just do you" mentality is thrown right out the window because, let's face it once you get a sober driver and a drunk passenger together, neither person is very tolerant. So where do we find the foundation for how to overcome such a prevailing and contrary political ideology?

The short answer is that it's in scripture. What I found to be absolutely amazing as I was doing research for this chapter of the book is just how balanced God is on this subject and just how much He has to say about it and who He sees as the responsible group to testify of the truth and the manner in which it should be broadcast. The Lord is very clear in the Bible about just how He expects us as Christians to behave as we share the truth to His creation. It is these expectations that should formulate the entire narrative of how we as a nation interact socially with one another.

The first principle that must be established as we look to redefine the social architecture of our great nation is that we must not desire to be offensive in the delivery of the truth. This must be the fundamental principle by which all subsequent principles are built upon. The moment we begin to speak the truth in a condescending tone, we almost immediately shut down respondents. They will become defensive and ignore the truth over saving face and salvaging their own personal dignities. Even as I was writing this book and sharing my ideas, I ran into this situation. As I was sharing my ideas of abortion with a fellow Christian, we were in complete agreement that abortion is wrong, but the moment I shared with him my thoughts on when life began his response was quick and harsh. "You do not possess the ability to properly discern scripture" is what I was told. Yet, when we were in agreement on the abortion issue as a whole, I was completely able to discern scripture. This is where the right is failing to gain ground in the area of social justice.

Why would anyone listen to someone who has no ability to learn and engage in debate only to hear his or her side of the argument broadcast? Proverbs 18:19 states, "A brother offended is harder to be won than a strong city: and contentions are like the bars of a castle." When we approach a dissenting argument with contention and offense, we actually imprison someone to continue to believe a lie. We have an obligation to remain humble in our approach to people of dissenting beliefs. Failing to do so only enables them to continue in the belief that we are hateful and therefore gives them cause to accuse us of being false. We must provide an atmosphere that will enable understanding and not contention. Psalm 119:104 says, "Through thy precepts I get understanding, therefore I hate every false way." How can we expect others to gain understanding if we share the truth in such a manner that they never hear the precept to begin with?

The Bible is full of verses that address the topic of a wise man being slow to anger. Proverbs 16:32 specifically addresses this concept: "He that is slow to anger is better than the mighty; and he that ruleth his spirit than he that taketh a city." The foundation of victory is not in meeting violence with violence but to meet aggression with a calm and very deliberate approach to understanding that we were once people who needed to be taught the truth. Ephesians 2:1-5 talks about how we, believers in Christ, were once dead in our own sins, yet we found grace in the eyes of God and He showed mercy toward us. Yet, now that we have the truth, we fail to remember just how much grace God extended toward us and do not show the same grace to other non-believers. We would be wise to remember this principle when addressing others whose world views differ from our own. Also, we must keep in mind that something caused them to believe what they believe. Just like something or someone is the reason you found the truth of the scriptures.

Another reason not to be offensive in our approach to discussions on social justice topics is the second principle of truth in the scriptures. The truth is offensive enough already. As a believer who attends church on a regular basis, I find it difficult to hear some of the truths written in God's word. This is because I am still human and fight against the flesh. The Apostle Paul wrote in Romans 7:14-17:

> "For we know that the law is spiritual: but I am carnal, sold under sin. For that which I do I allow not: for what I would, that do I not; but what I hate, that do I. If then I do that which I would not, I consent unto the law that it is good. Now then it is no more I that do it, but sin that dwelleth in me."

Paul is reminding us that we are all sinners, and it is the law that reminds us to not live in sin. At times, when we are reminded of the law, it conflicts with the flesh. That conflict of the truth of the law and the sin nature of the flesh can result in offense. So then if we as believers find offense with the law, how much more would those who do not believe? 1 Peter 1:7-8 makes this point very clear. I would ask every reader to take the time to search out the scriptures and truly exhaust this topic to see just how we have been missing the mark on reaching people with the truth simply by being too offensive in our approach.

So how do we avoid offending people when we are discussing such heated and deep rooted truths? The first step in presenting the truth without offense is to be consistent in our lives, living the truth in which we believe. In Titus 2:7-8 we are admonished to be incorruptible and show sincerity in our belief of the doctrine of scripture. Failing to be consistent in our beliefs can cause us to be a stumbling block to others. In Romans 14:12-17 we are given an example of a man who is offended by someone who eats meat. We are admonished not to eat meat in front of that person because doing so may cause a brother to fall. As bearers of the truth, when we approach others who do not have the truth, we should not be concerned with the fact that they lack the truth. That is exactly why we are there, to present it to them and do so with the intent to edify the person with whom we are sharing the truth.

Ephesians 4:29 states "Let no corrupt communication proceed out of your mouth, but that which is good to the use of edifying, that it may minister grace unto the hearer." Remember grace? That grace which was shown us before we knew the truth? In verse thirty-one of the same chapter we are told to "put away all bitterness, and wrath, and anger…" and to do so "with all malice." The only thing we are supposed to have malice toward is the bitterness, anger, and wrath in our own lives, not toward the imperfections of other's lives. And, in verse thirty-two it is clear we are to be kind toward each other, forgiving one another the way Christ has forgiven us. The love of Christ must be what shines through us as we share the truth with others.

1 Corinthians 13 is the gold standard by which our conversation and manifestation of our beliefs is measured. In the very first verse of this chapter the Apostle Paul writes to the church at Corinth, "Though I speak with the

tongues of men and angels, and have not charity, I am become as sounding brass, or a tinkling symbol." As I observe the current political pundit commentary, I cannot help but realize that all we are doing is making a whole bunch of noise. This is because we have the truth yet do not present it with charity toward the hearer and charity toward the true author of the truth, our Lord. What I see is people with the truth pounding on their desks, laughing at the people who disagree with them, calling the opposition names, and "owning" them (as many of the headers read on YouTube at least). Verses two and three continue to list a series of admirable character traits yet states that having these traits without charity profits nothing. Why are we not seeing greater gains made from the conservative movement on the social justice front? It is because we are not very charitable.

Another area of the social justice realm we are failing to make headway in is comparing our successes and failures to those of the opposition. An example of this is when a group of conservatives have a rally, and they get physical with opposing rally goers. The response usually looks something like, "Well, you ANTIFA folks aren't exactly saints yourselves." This serves absolutely no purpose toward furthering the acceptance of the truth to the nation at large. It is not our truth. It is God's truth, and He alone sets the standards for how His truth is to be presented. He also gives us a clear outline in scripture on how to make that happen. It does not matter how the opposition acts or reacts. We are only going to be judged on how we present the truth. End of story. The truth shared through our experiences.

The concept of comparative suffering, more commonly known as one-upmanship, is one way to express our experiences. However, this concept is divisive by nature. People or groups of people compete to determine who receives more benefits based on who has suffered more. This leads to someone or a group losing what they may have been initially entitled to due to comparative analysis. This way of thinking lacks compassion and denies people of rights and benefits afforded to them as citizens of this country.

Poor people say that a rich person doesn't know what real suffering is. The rich respond with "More money equals more problems." Neither group considers that each group has its share of struggles. Because the struggles are different they each draw the conclusion that the other is not struggling as much as they are. When our struggles are personal they tend to be more amplified. When we share one another's burdens, all struggles become personal. We then become more willing to help those who are struggling to find relief. In Proverbs 17: 17 we are told "a brother is born for adversity". In Genesis chapter six we are encouraged to bear one another's burdens.

Bearing one another's burdens is the biblical concept of shared experiences. In contrast, the comparative suffering, shared experience is inclusive in nature. It breeds understanding and develops empathy for one another's struggles. We relate to each other when we share the experience together. It also removes one of the greatest inhibitors to empathy: status, or class bigotry. The military has a firm grasp on this concept.

The institution of the shared experience concept becomes apparent to a new military recruit the moment he or she first steps foot on the drill pad at any military basic training base. Drill Instructors begin shouting commands at the recruits, creating chaos right from the start. Every recruit is in a state of panic and confusion. Recruits who fail to comply with the commands are given special attention and further motivation in the form of the Drill Instructor repeating the command. This is followed by more colorful words describing the recruit's inability to follow simple instructions. All of this takes place with the drill instructor knowing the recruit is not stupid and the instructions given were not simple. The drill instructor has done what he or she has set out to do: create an environment that will challenge the recruits and require them to deny selfish interest for the good of the group. Everyone in basic training will suffer together and through this shared experience will grow to help each other succeed and earn one another's respect.

Units such as the Special Forces, Navy S.E.A.L.s, and the Army Rangers add an additional component to this concept. They receive a title and an adornment to recognize their achievement, which is a testimony to all who see of their shared experiences manifesting into a brotherhood. For the Special Forces, it is a green beret. For the S.E.A.L.s, it is a trident. And for the Army Rangers, it is a tan beret. The U.S. Marine Corps takes great pride in earning the Eagle, Globe, and Anchor. These are the observable, repeatable and measurable truths that prove shared experiences are more productive to a society than comparative suffering.

The final principle in presenting truth is that we are not to be offended by the opposition. If we are asking the opposition to stop being so sensitive and easily offended, we ourselves must not be so sensitive and easily offended. Psalm 119:165 says, "Great peace have they which love thy law: and nothing shall offend them." We say we have the truth. Our peace comes from knowing that truth. If we say we have the truth, then we should not be offended by the opposing view. If I got a question wrong on a test in school, the teacher was not offended that I was wrong. He or she would continue to share the truth of the subject with me until I grasped it. If we get offended and respond with contention, it inhibits the communication process and no one learns anything. This sentiment is further illustrated in Proverbs 13:10 where it says, "Only by pride cometh contention: but with the well advised is wisdom."

We are given the perfect example of the truth being presented, the individual rejecting the truth, and the presenter not getting offended. Wouldn't you know? Christ himself is the example in this story. In Matthew 19:16-22 we read the story of the rich young ruler asking Christ what he must do to have eternal life. Christ tells him to obey the commandments, to which the rich man says he has kept them from his youth. Then Christ says (paraphrasing) since you have been perfect, go and sell everything and give to the poor and take up your cross and follow me. The rich young ruler, we are told, went away sorrowful because he was a very rich man. This man was in the presence of truth itself yet did not believe. What in this great world would ever make us think we have the power to convince anyone to change their minds? Christ himself could not do it. That is the power of free will. God gave it to man, and not even Christ can take it away. Seriously, we need to let that truth sink in deeply. It will change the way in which we approach our conversations regarding the passionate topics we find in the social justice arena.

What does the manifestation of these principles look like in the real world (our modern political climate)? The one example I am going to use is extreme, one that tends to be very offensive to the Christian right. To show the world what the love of Christ looks like manifested in real time toward real people. If we say God is our Creator, we must then acknowledge that He created all of the people who hold opposing views. They are just as fearfully and wonderfully made. So the example I am going to use is that of the preferred pronouns ideology of the transgender community. As I engage a member of the transgender community in a discussion on my beliefs, and they prefer to be called a pronoun inconsistent with their assigned gender at birth, I have no issue doing it. Just as the Apostle Paul showed us in the example of not eating meat in front of one who sees the eating of meat as offensive.

This does not mean I have to agree with their lifestyle or agenda. It just means I meet them in the condition they are, just as Christ met me: a sinner in need of a Savior. Christ did not become a pimp in order to reach prostitutes. Neither did He shame them. He presented the truth and let the Holy Spirit do his job. There is only one entity that can convince men and women of wrong doing and not of them are in the Republican Party. We read in John 16, the only entity that has the authority to convince mankind of sin is the Holy Spirit. So, if you are not him, you don't get to act offended if people don't change their minds when you speak to them. Our job is to tell the truth and allow the Holy Spirit to work. You never know, the love you share today may be the conversion of tomorrow.

A personal story I have about this very topic is when our church was out in the city of Copperas Cove, TX inviting people to our church. It was a Sunday evening, and we were knocking on doors in a neighborhood close to our church. I had just finished handing out fliers on one street and was heading back down the street to where I was to meet the bus and head back to church. As I was walking back down the street there was a lesbian couple heading in the opposite direction. I was not wearing a suit and tie, but I did have on slacks and a short sleeved, collared shirt. With a stack of church fliers in my hand, it was clear what I was doing there. They kept their heads forward but their eyes would glance over at me every once in a while. That look of "please don't come over and talk to me" filled both of their faces with dreaded anticipation. So, with eager enthusiasm, I made my way toward them.

The lady who was closest to me already had one hand out in the way a traffic cop does to signify traffic to stop moving forward. To disarm her just a little, I gave as welcome a smile as I could and said, "I am not here to sell you anything." She responded with a half grin and a "We don't do that" response, knowing that what I was handing her was a gospel tract with the plan of salvation on it. I responded with "Ma'am, I just want to give you this gift and invite y'all to our church just up the road." To which she responded "Like we'd be welcome?" My response was simple and direct: "Now who is judging whom? I promise you this, if you and your partner show up tonight, there will be two seats waiting for you. And I will be there to meet you at the front door." Her response was just as simple and direct.

She just smiled a soft but genuine smile. It said thanks but no thanks. And she and her partner walked away. She did take the tract and with it the plan of salvation. She walked away with the truth in her hand. If I had taken offense to their relationship, the only guarantee that day would have been that they would have never taken the tract and had the opportunity to read the truth. And, just maybe, because of the love extended to her and her partner that day, she will be more receptive to the truth in the future. I love that God allowed me to experience that moment in those women's lives. When Christians take the lead and begin to collectively treat people the way Christ has instructed them to, it will prevent the government from ever believing it needs to get involved in regulating our social behavior.

7

JESUS IS NOT A SOCIALIST

> *"And thou shalt not glean thy vineyard, neither shalt thou gather every grape of thy vineyard; Thou shalt leave them for the poor and stranger: I am the Lord your God."*
>
> Leviticus 19:10

I will have to admit, Chapter Six was going to be the final chapter of this book. I really had no desire to even discuss the subject of socialism. The primary reason for me not wanting to address this topic is that socialism is such an epic failure of a political discipline. I really didn't think it was worth investing my time to discuss such a failed ideology. What changed my mind was the narrative that seemed to be flooding social media as I was writing the previous chapters to this book. "Jesus is a Socialist" memes seemed to be popping up everywhere. This has become the defense of left-wing politics in an attempt to combat the conservative economic world view of a free market. It is a vain attempt at shaming God fearing Americans into accepting socialism as a viable form of governance.

As quoted above, Leviticus 19:10 is the verse most used in these memes meant to prove that Christ is indeed a socialist. The problem with this narrative of Christ's assumed political world view is not just that it is false; it is also that the medium by which this information is given lacks maturity of thought and depth of understanding. An extreme departure from the prevailing wisdom of this topic could never be fully expressed with a simple picture of Jesus holding a baby while sheep gather at his feet and a single verse quoting God's intentions as to how to care for the less fortunate members in society. These simple memes only serve to evoke emotions in an attempt to sway the reader into believing the desired narrative. If we won't agree with socialism, they want us to feel guilty about it. In this chapter, I will provide the maturity of thought and depth of understanding this particular subject matter needs in order to draw the proper conclusion on what God's intention is for His creation as it pertains to governance at the national level. I will answer the question of whether or not Jesus truly is a socialist.

The Bottom Line Up Front (BLUF): Is Christ a Socialist? The short answer is no. Don't go getting too excited there, Republicans. As we begin to delve deep into the understanding of how our Creator God has designed things, we are going to see just how far off both political parties have been in regards to caring for those who are truly less fortunate than others. God never intended for any nation to have a supreme ruler to govern entire nations. His desire was for the individual citizens of each nation to simply follow his truths, apply his principles, and worship him as their Creator. This intent is shown in 1Samuel,

Chapter Eight. The people of Israel had turned their backs on God. The two sons of the Judge, Samuel, had abandoned their faith and were not following after God. So, in rebellion, the people of Israel went to Samuel and asked for God to grant them a king to rule over them.

Samuel approached God with the request of the people. God warned Samuel that in taking a king and not following God, there would be dire consequences. They would forfeit their lands, their daughters, and individual rights for the will of the government. They would be required to use their labor to support unjust wars. Not just by sending their fathers to fight the wars, but also the labor back home in making the instruments of war. The warning: by taking on a large government representative to make the laws to rule over you, you forfeit your individual liberties and are subject to the whim of the man or woman in charge. Even after Samuel issued God's warning to the Israelite's, they still wanted a king appointed to rule over them. It does not take great depth of research to see how both political parties have adopted this same mentality when it comes to big government rule.

I like to remind my republican friends that it was a republican who removed us from the "Gold Standard" of economic strength and even went so far as to enact wage and price controls in an attempt to control inflation. If that is not big government, I don't know what is. And then of course, there is the left. At least they admit they are for big government. This gives the opposition a means by which to address the issues with their political world view. Hence, we have the reason for the penning of this chapter. The republicans also use big government tactics, like gerrymandering, to manipulate voter population characteristics. Citizens allowing a large government to manipulate how it represents its constituents leave those being represented at the mercy of the representatives. The larger the government becomes the less individual liberties the citizenry has. God literally warns of this in 1 Samuel Chapter Eight.

So, why does individual liberty even exist? For what reason did God give us free will to begin with? In Genesis Chapter One the Bible says we are created in the image of God. Being created in His image, we also possess many of His qualities. Among these qualities is the ability to demonstrate love as well as justice. Furthermore, God granted us the authority to exercise these qualities over the whole earth. It is our responsibility to exercise these qualities with wisdom and understanding. We must heed the warnings from our Creator to ensure that we demonstrate His great love and justice to the world. It is His creation and therefore His rules apply. He has warned us of the difficulties of big government having rule over people. He squarely places the authority on the individual to behave in concert with the truths and principles written in His word.

Why did God set His creation up this way? What is the benefit of having individual responsibility over collective rule? With individual responsibility, greater success is achieved. This is due to the greatest byproduct of individuality: dignity. Dignity leads to self-worth, and that leads to the success of the community. It does not take a community to raise a child. It takes parents raising a child to produce a productive member of the community. Socialism puts the cart before the horse. Conservatives would then have you believe that making laws limiting human behavior are then striping away the rights of the individual, rights that were clearly endowed by the Creator.

This is also a misrepresentation of the truth. Establishing laws that dictate human behavior are not against God's principles of governance, especially when we are talking about how we care for the less fortunate of our society.

One of the very first principles we see in the Bible concerning the poor is that they will always be a part of society. In Matthew 26:11, when Jesus was rebuking His disciples for their judgment over the sinful woman who anoints Jesus's feet with precious ointment, He says, "For ye have the poor with you always; but me ye have not always." I have written the entire verse here to avoid misinterpreting scripture and to keep the verse in its context. Christ, in this passage, is not directly addressing the issue of poverty but is referencing the fact that there will always be people in need within our societies. Our job is not to concern ourselves with the riches of this world to get gain for the sake of riches, but to use those riches to worship God and display the love of Christ to a lost and dying world.

While the story of the sinful woman is not about politics, within it is a great principle we can apply. A poor woman has a portion of wealth in the form of valuable oil. The treasurer of the disciples, Judas, rebukes the woman for wasting the oil when he could have sold and used the money to help the poor. It is here that Jesus offers the response mentioned in the previous paragraph concerning the poor. The treasurer, in this story, sought to redistribute the wealth for the sake of helping more poor. What Christ perceived was the heart of the one attempting to take from one to give to others. He perceived the heart was deceitful and was merely using the idea of helping the poor as a way of shaming the one who was poor to begin with. When we hear our politicians make claims of taking wealth from others to redistribute "for the greater good," be reminded of this story. Then, seek to understand the heart of the one asking society to take more from the individual than it is willing to give of itself.

I must reiterate that I am not taking the above mentioned story out of context. This story is not about politics. However, the principle of redistribution of wealth is demonstrated in this passage of scripture. It can be applied to how we govern ourselves and ensure we do so wisely. The principle is this: If national leadership is asking for its citizens to give up their wealth for the greater good, we as a society need to determine what is driving them to ask us to sacrifice in such a way. If it proves to be deceitful, it is then wrong to give up that wealth. The way in which we can validate the heart of this request is to ask our leaders if they will subject themselves to the same law. If they will not, it is then clear that they do not truly believe in that of which they are asking their constituents to commit.

The best example of this is in the city of Seattle, Washington. Three of the richest men live in or around this city, and they give substantial amounts of money to causes they believe in. They are seen as very philanthropic individuals. They have also been champions for the socialist ideas for redistribution of wealth, yet in that same city, they keep their businesses subject to tax incentives and class segregation. They are wealthy and are going to live in a wealthy city where they can live separately from the less fortunate. There are currently over 12,500 people in Seattle who are homeless. How can this be? Three billionaires who believe in redistribution of wealth all live in this city. They speak of the great utopia that is created through redistributing wealth, yet there are still homeless people and families in their "great" city. This situation echoes the principles written in the story of the sinful woman and the alabaster box. Namely, there will always be poor people in our society, but if there are those among you asking to redistribute your wealth and are unwilling to abide by the same laws, the truth is not in them and they are deceiving you.

There are over two-thousand verses in the Bible that dictate how to treat the poor and needy. There are less than fifty verses that discuss the way in which a poor man is to treat the "rich." I put "rich" in quotations because many of those verses talk more about the employee to boss relationship in which the employee works for his master and needs to be a diligent worker. Proverbs 14:31 says, "He that oppresseth the poor reproaches his maker: but he that honoureth him hath mercy on the poor." You want to honor the Lord? Show mercy to the poor. In the book of Deuteronomy, chapter 24, we are told not to take advantage of the poor when we hire them. That means we cannot say to the poor, "I will pay you less than the normal wage because you are poor." They deserve fair wages.

If it is not big government's responsibility to assist with caring for the poor, whose responsibility is it? The answer is three-tiered. The first tier is this: There does need to be big government oversight. In scripture we see this in the character of God. He established the rules and principles of life. Then, by granting us free will, He delegated to us the authority and responsibility to rule with wisdom. God is our overseer and the ultimate authority, yet the success of His established rules is up to us to govern effectively by applying His principles and heeding His warnings. Here in America our Constitution was set up to be the overseer by which all other state rights would be answerable to. This is consistent with how our Creator established principles of governance. Then, we as the residents of any given state, through the democratic process, get to select those who we wish to represent us at the national level. There, these selected representatives write bills to enact laws on our behalf. We as a country do well when applying these principles to criminal behavior but abandon them when it comes to social programs.

In Deuteronomy we see the first laws being established, and among those laws are provisions to care for the poor and their needs. In Chapter 24, verses 19-21 we see the first example of the gleaning of the fields provision. With this provision, farmers and vineyard owners were instructed to leave the portions of the harvest that fell to the ground to the stranger, the fatherless, and the widow. They were told not to return to the field and pick up what was left behind. This was done for two reasons: To remember they were once slaves in Egypt and to show their obedience to God, and God would bless the work of their hands. In the book of Leviticus we see this provision become much more deliberate in its execution. Here they are told not to harvest the corners of their fields, but to leave these corners as well as the harvest which fell to the ground. God demands we have compassion on those in need. Our obedience to His law proves that we love Him and have compassion for His creation. It is in these above mentioned laws that we see this responsibility is given to local businesses. They were told to assist the poor with provisions from their harvest.

Does the local government have any responsibility in caring for the poor? What does the bible say about the church's responsibilities in this matter? Well, these are not clearly defined responsibilities in scripture. That is to say, there is no direct verse that states, "The church shall care for the poor." Nor is there any verse that states, "Regional governors and/or council members shall enact laws providing for the poor." There are some principles written in scripture that allude to these organizations and political authority's responsibilities to the poor. The inference to the church is in the letters the Apostle Paul wrote to the church. He speaks of assisting the poor as a way of testifying to the love of Christ with the ultimate goal of salvation of the lost as the reason for obedience in this matter.

As far as local government involvement as it pertains to scripture, I admit that what I am about to share is a bit of a stretch. However, I also feel that the example provided by Old Testament Israel certainly serves as a good model for enacting and enforcing laws at the state, regional, and local levels.

Israel was divided into twelve tribes. God appointed leaders of those twelve tribes to conduct their first census. Here we see the Lord delegating authority and responsibility to lower leadership for the execution of His laws. Then, when Israel continued to disobey the Lord, He established the rule of law through the judges. These judges were rulers whom God used to defeat Israel's enemies as well as maintain Jewish law among the Israelites. While not having a direct mandate, these examples show how God has used local government representation and the church to provide for His creation.

There is one caveat to the redistribution of wealth concept mentioned earlier in this chapter. This caveat comes by way of the tribe of Levi. God had mandated that the tribe of Levi would not receive the inheritance of Israel. Rather, God would be their inheritance. This was unique due to the relationship God would have with the Levites and the work they were required to do in the Temple. Here we see another example of the redistribution of wealth concept in scripture. The remaining eleven tribes were instructed to bring the tithes of their increases to the gates every three years. The Levites, strangers, fatherless, and widows were allowed to take of these tithes for their livelihood. What is important to notice here is the "why" behind this principle. Why is the redistribution taking place? It was established for the purpose of helping those who have nothing to the obedience of God for the testimony of the great love of Christ. If redistribution is happening for any other reason, the process will fail.

In summation: Is Christ a Socialist? We have seen how God warned of the dangers of big government and never intended for Israel to have a king. We see in scripture how God has delegated His authority to man to have dominion over this world and to rule it with wisdom. This demonstrates His love and justice to His creation though individual effort. We see how God has mandated that we set our increase aside to help the poor. He requires it of the individual, not the government. However, while there is no direct mandate that the local government or churches care for the poor, God has shown us though His own example how effective local government can be at caring for its people. This cannot be stated enough. God used the delegation to the local tribes to execute His laws. They had the individual responsibility to manage their tribes. Each then gave an account for their actions. The result might affect the nation as a whole, yes; but God did not change the law simply because one tribe did not obey.

The greatest benefit to establishing a government that is run on these Biblical principles is that it provides the best opportunity for the greatest successes we can have in our society. These principles develop individual dignity through the freedom of individual accomplishment. That means, as long as I apply these principles–regardless of my race, color, sexual orientation, or religious belief–I will be successful. This does not mean the results will be the same for every person. One person may end up a millionaire while another may have to wait until he or she is sixty-five to retire. But a successful life was lived. Not a life free of challenges but free to allow the individual's efforts to affect the outcome. For Christians, our testimony should draw others to Christ. For non-believers, they get to count their toys at the end. Also, this system of government provides hope. Hope that I can work myself out of poverty. If I can't, at least I have a community that cares for me and will help meet my needs.

This system delegates the responsibility for action to the lowest level of government. This ensures that the people who need assistance get it when the need arises. If I am an elected official and am given the authority to provide assistance to the poor in my district, I will be more apt to help knowing these people now have a reason to keep me in office. If I fail to help those in need, my chances of getting reelected are much slimmer. For example, if we empowered local government to provide for the care of its poor and needy, and an elected official in charge of ensuring the financial requirements of his or her community failed to do so, that person would stand a better chance of not getting reelected. The result is that power is then given to the people, not the elected official. Then, with the assistance provided, the elected official ensures the person who uses the assistance does so with the intent to improve their station in the community.

If for any reason the people in need are unable to improve their station in life, they may be placed on a different form of assistance. Rather than monetary assistance, they may be placed in a community shelter. There are many ways in which this could manifest itself. The ultimate goal is that individuals in the community have the authority to act in a way that ensures the best outcome for the community while providing for the needs of those less fortunate. For those who are against this form of government, I agree that this is not perfect and for the reasons you say it's not.

It relies on the benevolence of the people. It also relies on people in leadership positions to ensure, with honesty and integrity, the execution of these laws. And that is the biggest flaw in the system. It relies on the generosity of the individual. We know that there will be wealthy people lacking generosity. Therefore, people will go hungry. People will go without shelter or a place to conduct personal hygiene. All these things are true. So, what does the Bible say about this? God will execute judgment against those who are rich and fail to assist with the care of His creation. My job is to do what I can and help in ways God enables me to, not demand that my neighbor do the same. Returning to the Seattle example, three billionaires live in one city. There are over 12,500 homeless people living there. If those billionaires, who believe in redistribution of wealth, will not pull their resources to provide for the homeless in their own city, they don't have the right to take one dollar from me when I have homeless in my own city where I am trying to help.

Now that the biblical laws and principles have been listed and the pros and cons established, how do these ideas manifest in our system of government? It will first require us to rethink how we should assist those in need and the manner in which that assistance is provided. The manner is simple enough. It should be delegated to the lowest possible level of government, leaving the federal government as an overseer to ensure that programs are executed with integrity. That would mean any current federal assistance programs would cease. Programs like Medicare would no longer be needed. Before you throw the book at the wall, I need you to keep reading to allow these ideas to mature. As I said at the beginning of this chapter, it is going to take depth of understanding, which was provided in the first half of this chapter, and maturity of thought. This is where we apply that concept. The foundation for us to truly help the poor will begin with a reduction in federal taxes and the institution of a flat tax rate with federal taxes only going to the fifteen cabinet positions providing oversight for government funded programs. This flat tax rate would exempt people whose individual income is $35,000 or less, annually.

With the fifteen cabinet positions of the executive branch being the basis for all oversight for government funded programs, there becomes a one-stop-shop of responsibility for federal funding issues. For example, an underprivileged school in Detroit needs assistance buying updated school books for the new school year. The local school district petitions the city for funding and they provide what they can, but it does not meet the funding requirements to purchase new books for the entire school. The school then has fundraising events throughout the summer, hosted by the city, and is able to raise more funds but again comes up short. They can then petition the department of education for federal funds to assist with meeting the required funds to provide for the people of Detroit.

One of the pillars of this tax plan to assist with the poor would require an increase in state and local taxes. This might manifest itself in higher sales or property taxes. It would be left to the people to vote on how they want to be taxed in order to meet the needs of their communities. To meet the needs of the homeless, federal oversight might go to the Department of Housing and Urban Development (HUD), but the funding for the local community will be done through taxes at the state and local level, keeping the money from that community there to assist the people of that community with tax laws voted on by people of that community. All of this would be executed with checks and balances for proper execution provided by the people of that community through the voting process. Now those representatives would have actual incentives to truly work for and represent their constituents. With the decrease in federal taxes paid by the American people, they would be able to absorb the increase in taxes at the state and local level.

Another pillar of this program is the allowing of local communities to determine the level of financial responsibility verses time given to assist with helping the poor. This would allow communities to determine whether they want to give more of their time rather than their money. This could manifest itself by way of adopting an organization type programs. This is where a few companies or other non-profit organizations give of their time through volunteering to help keep the tax burden down. For example, Companies A, B, and C decide they have employees that will volunteer–between the three of them–forty hours a week to serve food and clean the facilities of a food service provider to the poor. And, other companies and non-profits are able to commit to other community assistance programs to reduce the tax burden on the local community. Imagine: a community using the strength of the individuals to ensure the success of the community. Now imagine an elected official actually representing his or her constituents in a way the constituents voted for.

Another pillar to add to the success of this program would be to allow states to tailor the program based on population density. More rural states like Wyoming, the Dakotas, and Montana might only need oversight down to the state level. The tax requirements in these states might also be much less. This is another win for the free market. This provides businesses and people incentive to want to live in smaller communities. Larger cities could be further divided into districts or even housing developments. An example of this would be New York City. The city is already broken down into five separate boroughs. These boroughs could serve as separate tax districts, then funding from taxes collected in each borough could go back into that district to help the larger community. Keep in mind the overarching principle of allowing the states to determine what those tax districts look like for each state. The same method of raising funds for any shortcoming in the tax cycle as discussed in the Department of Education example a few paragraphs earlier could then be applied.

I am a conservative who believes in social programs. I do not believe big government is where they should be managed. The Lord has a very clear blueprint for how we are to care for the poor and needy among us. He delegates the authority to us as His creation to enact laws that are in keeping with His principles and show the world that we are obedient to Him. If we who say we believe God do not act in accordance with His will when it comes to the care of those less fortunate, then Socialism will always have a voice in our political discussions. If we wish to silence our detractors, we must do so with action by showing them we do believe in God and will act in accordance with His principles to care for His creation.

8

Conclusion

> *"Get wisdom, get understanding: forget it not; neither decline from the words of my mouth. Forsake her not, and she shall preserve thee: love her, and she shall keep thee. Wisdom is the principle thing; therefor get wisdom: and with all thy getting get understanding"*
>
> Proverbs 4:5 – 7

The leaders of our nation are known for making empty promises. Political satirists make a living on this premise. On one hand, we as citizens of this great country have accepted the idea of untrustworthy politicians as business as usual. On the other hand, we brag about how great our country is and then complain when our leaders fail to deliver on the promises of their political campaigns. Our leadership is inconsistent with the way in which they govern. The result is a voter base that is inconsistent with the way it desires to be governed.

We seem to be–at least since I have been following politics (and I have been following since President Carter)–on an eight year political cycle. We, as the voters of our leadership, become disillusioned with the incumbent leadership and its political party. During the next election cycle we vow to vote for a leader who will bring sweeping changes to the status quo. As a constituency we grant this party and its leaders four years to accomplish the changes they promised on the campaign trail. During those four years we are placated by the useless platitudes of these politicians in hope they will win the next election and be able to make all of the real, sweeping changes they promised us during the first election.

We go through all of this, only to live through another four years in disbelief as we watch the ones we trusted to run our country still failing to deliver on their promises. And, once their failures are finally realized, they spend the first two years post-transition deflecting those failures onto the other political party. "If I just had the cooperation of bipartisanship, I could have really made an impact." Then, after we have lost faith in that candidate and his or her party, we switch party loyalties in hopes of getting the change we voted for in the previous eight years. Then again, we end up never getting the true changes this nation deserves. Or, maybe we are getting exactly what we deserve, and this system plays out every eight years. We have, without a doubt, the finest system of government this world has ever seen. Our problem is that we lack leadership with a firm foundation by which decisions are made.

The previous chapters of this book discussed some of the most divisive topics of our current political climate. The intent of this book was to show how biblical truths and principles, when applied correctly, can manifest free of partiality to a given political agenda. Having a foundation for decision making built on immovable truth eliminates the moral dilemma. This characteristic is essential for leaders to be successful. It provides trusted consistency in leadership from the people they seek to lead. If leaders are inconsistent in decision making, they are untrustworthy. James 1:8 says, "A double minded man is unstable in all his ways." A moral foundation prevents this instability.

The two main political parties, Republicans and Democrats, fail to achieve political effectiveness because both are unstable in all their ways. The Left has compassion. That, at least, is the narrative to the people. Yet, it lacks wisdom in adopting a viable solution to care for those truly in need. The Right does love that we are a nation of laws, yet it lacks the compassion to extend mercy to people in need simply because the law says, "You committed this offense; you deserve the harshness of prison." There is no real means provided for rehabilitation prior to an offender's return to society. The Left blames liberal politics on why recidivism rates are so high.

In 1 Corinthians 13, the Apostle Paul tells us that we can do every great thing in the world, but if we don't have charity it profits us nothing. We can create laws, sign executive orders, taut our political rhetoric on social media in hopes we change people's minds, but if we do not do it out of love for God's creation, these actions will fail. In Matthew 9:36-38, Jesus saw the multitude and was moved with compassion. He then challenged His disciples to pray that God would send workers to meet the needs of others. This book has provided ways in which we as voters should demand our leaders think and behave in order to meet the needs of the citizens of our great country.

Because I have used the Bible as the foundation for decision making when it comes to national interest, many will say, "You can't make me believe in your God. Our constitution ensures separation of church and state. No religious document can be used to establish laws in our country." My response to these statements is very simple: You are right. I cannot make you believe in my God. As a born again Christian, it is my desire that all would come to the saving knowledge of Jesus Christ, but I do not possess the power to make that happen. There is only one entity that can convince men of their sin, and I am not Him. But that does not mean that the application of these principles will not bring about the desired results in decision making.

To further illustrate this point I would like to provide an example using aviation. [13]According to the FAA there are 2.7 million passengers that fly on commercial airlines, daily. I am going to make a bold assumption that fifty percent of these passengers could not list the five major laws of physics or the four basic principles of aerodynamics. Their belief in them, regardless of where these truths even come from, or even their complete ignorance of them is irrelevant to the success of the application of these truths. Yet every day, millions of unbelievers get on airplanes all over the United States and are subject to these laws and principles whether or not they like it. For the pilots, those who do believe must understand the laws and apply the principles or the results could be disastrous. We as a society have already demonstrated that we have the capacity to trust others who believe something or know something we do not and then place our lives in their hands as demonstration of that trust.

---

[13] https://www.faa.gov/air_traffic/by_the_numbers/

CONCLUSION

I will concede there is a very important variable missing from the above example: precedence. Anyone who boards a commercial airplane today does so with the foreknowledge that planes have flown and made it to their destination safely, so the faith demonstrated by the modern air traveler is not blind. It just so happens we have historical precedence concerning a nation establishing its laws on the laws and principles of governance established in the Bible. When Israel applied them, they were successful. When they did not, they found themselves in captivity. We look to the past for the failures of socialism and can determine that that system of governance never leads to the rescue of the impoverished.

The application of the principles discussed in this book will result in the successful inclusion of all God's creation. How do I know? Because it is God who established them. You see, a transgender soldier can serve as long as the transition process does not affect readiness because negatively effecting readiness can result in injury or, worse, loss of life to many other soldiers. Here we have an example of how laws can be applied with compassion for all. That does not mean everyone gets what they want, but everyone has the opportunity to be a productive member of society. My hope is that this book encourages American voters to change the way they see politics in our country. They would renew their commitment to gain understanding of the real issues we face as a nation and would demand that leaders who are running for office adopt immovable principles based on the laws and principles of God. After all, it is the future of our country that is as stake.

REFERENCES

- All scripture references are from the *King James Version Bible*, digital application, app3daily, updated 20 October 2019
- The Endowment for Human Development, Prenatal Form and Function – *The Making of an Earth Suit* (on-line article)
- Cunningham FG, MacDonald PC, Gant NF, et al. 1997. *Williams Obstetrics, 20th ed.* Stamford: Appleton and Lange.
- ABC News, Third Presidential Debate, 19 October 2016
- 18 U.S. Code § 1111. Murder
- Law.com
- Forbes Article, *Are American Taxpayers Paying for Abortion?*, 2 October 2005
- Penn Wharton, UPENN, Budget Model, *The Effects of Immigration on the United Sates' Economy*, 27 January 2016
- *Immigration's Effects on the Economy and You*, Kimberly Amadeo, 25 January 2019
- *Inside Elizabeth Warren's grassroots strategy*, MJ Lee, 15 March 2019

REFERENCES

- Durose, Matthew R., Alexia D. Cooper, and Howard N. Snyder, *Recidivism of Prisoners Released in 30 States in 2005: Patterns from 2005 to 2010*, Bureau of Justice Statistics Special Report, April 2014, NCJ 244205.
- Chris TrotterMonash University, Australia, *Reducing Recidivism Through Probation Supervision: What We Know and Don't Know From Four Decades of Research,* September 2013.
- Steven Yoder, Pacific Standard Staff, *What's the Real Rate of Sex-Crime Recidivism,* 14 June 2017
- https://www.faa.gov/air_traffic/by_the_numbers/

Made in the USA
Las Vegas, NV
25 November 2020